MW01265599

THE
POWER
OF **WINNING**
THINKING

THE
POWER
OF WINNING
THINKING

Living Life Successfully During Good Times and Bad

FRANS M.J. BRANDT

Copyright © 2009 by Frans M.J. Brandt.

Library of Congress Control Number: 2009907901
ISBN: Hardcover   978-1-4415-6142-8
                    Softcover   978-1-4415-6141-1

Important Notice

This book presents a general overview and is not a substitute for professional advice. When faced with a mental, physical, social, vocational, or any other personal or interpersonal problem, it is necessary to seek personalized professional assistance.

All rights reserved.

No part of this publication may be reproduced, stored in a retrieval system, or transmitted in any form, by any means, without the written permission of the copyright holder.

© 2009 by Frans M. J. Brandt, EdD, LPC, LMFT

Book cover by Annette J. Blair.

This book was printed in the United States of America.

To order additional copies of this book, contact:
Xlibris Corporation
1-888-795-4274
www.Xlibris.com
Orders@Xlibris.com
63554

Contents

Preface 7

PART ONE
Winners Have A Winning Attitude

1   A Winning Attitude Is Needed for Lasting Success 11
2   A Winning Attitude Has Three Essential Traits 14

PART TWO
Winners Have A Winning Personality

3   Winners Are Adaptable 23
4   Winners Are Ageless 26
5   Winners Are Altruistic 37
6   Winners Are Assertive 41
7   Winners Are Committed 45
8   Winners Are Competent.. 48
9   Winners Are Consistent 51
10 Winners Are Content... 54
11 Winners Are Cooperative 59
12 Winners Are Courageous 63
13 Winners Are Disciplined 70
14 Winners Are Doers.. 74
15 Winners Are Enthusiastic 79
16 Winners Are Grateful... 82
17 Winners Are Honest 84
18 Winners Are Motivated.. 87
19 Winners Are Role Models... 90

20 Winners Are Successful 95
21 Winners Are Tenacious.. 98

PART THREE
Winners Have Wholesome Goals

22 Winners Have a Healthy Social Conscience........................ 105
23 Winners Have a Healthy Reverence for Life 109
24 Winners Have a Healthy Personality Style......................... 113
25 Winners Have a Healthy Physical Lifestyle........................ 118
26 Winners Have a Healthy Emotional Outlook 129
27 Winners Have a Healthy Philosophy of Life 142

Epilogue 149

References.. 163

Index (Names) 167

Index (Subjects).. 171

Preface

As I write this preface, most of the world's nations—including our own—are being assaulted daily by extraordinary cultural, economic, and social upheavals. Although we may be influenced by these and other historical events, it is good to know that, ultimately, we still write our own personal history. I am firmly convinced that we feel and live in accordance with the habitual manner by which we think. A recent massive economic and financial downturn—in the making for decades—found many individuals financially and mentally unprepared. This has led to a rise in depression, suicide, violence, and many other sad events. Yet in the midst of all the negative news, this book comes with the positive message that *we can* have a meaningful life during both good times and bad!

In my professional work during the past four decades, I have had ample opportunity to observe that most human beings can alter their attitudes and, thus, transform their lives. I have witnessed how one motivated person after another was able to turn his or her life around, learning to switch from hopelessness to hope, sadness to joy, and sickness to health. The varied challenges that brought these individuals into my office nearly always proved far less crucial than their readiness to change from self-defeating (faulty) thinking to constructive (winning) thinking. Each of these individuals required specific remedial strategies. However, none of these could have been successfully implemented without each person's full commitment to embrace *winning thinking: a powerful fusion of realism with reason and optimism.*

If there is anything that explicitly characterizes human beings, it is found in their thought-life. All of us are unmistakably defined by our thoughts and beliefs and, even more so, by our attitudes. The book of Proverbs quite eloquently reminds us that "pleasant words are like honey; sweet to the mind and health to the body," and, even more vividly, "death and life is in the power of the tongue." And this also is the fundamental message embedded in every page of this book: *think right, and you will feel and live right!* The power of the tongue reflects our thought-life, which is either good or bad for us; there is no third choice. Regrettably, all too many people overlook the far-reaching "power of the tongue" and find themselves deeply entangled in faulty-thinking and self-defeating lifestyles. This book, among other things, seeks to awaken an often-dormant power: the power to wisely choose our own destiny. Presently, there is a *dire need* for winning thinking and making wise choices as America faces unprecedented challenges in employment, finance, health care, public safety, and social stability in general.

Perhaps at no other time in the history of this country has it been more requisite to heed the habitual manner in which we think and live. In addition to employment, financial, and other social challenges, there are other urgent issues that demand our full attention. The sober realization that 75-85 percent of all mental and physical health challenges—including cancer, depression, diabetes, and heart disease—are preventable, should give us pause to consider our customary mode of thinking and living.

The Power of Winning Thinking not only describes the three primary and most commonly found secondary characteristics of *authentic winners*, but also mentions dozens of these individuals by name. It has been known throughout the ages that our attitudes propel us through life and set the course of our destiny. The good news is that most of us truly have a choice in this matter. "YES, WE CAN" is far more than a political slogan. It is a powerful reality for those who choose to fully embrace and practice WINNING THINKING!

PART ONE

WINNERS HAVE A WINNING ATTITUDE

1

A Winning Attitude Is Needed
for Lasting Success

A winner is a solution-focused person with a winning attitude, who, in the pursuit of a wholesome goal, will get up one more time, every time. This definition makes a clear distinction between those who *appear* to be winners and those who *are* winners. Many individuals who seem to be winners are all too often only self-serving individuals. The mind-set of real winners, however, is not focused on egotism. Yes, they are ambitious and assertive, but they are also caring, compassionate, and cooperative. They have *wholesome goals* that may include such values as a social conscience, reverence for life and selfless love. Every well-known authentic winner in the history of this country pursued wholesome goals.

How Attitudes Are Acquired

Attitudes are habitual predispositions that have taken a long time to acquire. Thus, if someone habitually reacts in a negative manner, it is useless to think that this person can instantly change that particular behavior permanently. To acquire a new attitude takes both time and effort. It requires that we think about and regularly practice the new thoughts and beliefs that are to replace old ones. With consistent practice and determination, however, these new thoughts and beliefs will eventually become attitudes.

In childhood and early adolescence, our attitudes were primarily formed through classical conditioning when we learned to associate

11

one thing with another. For example, a smile might mean safety, while a frown might indicate danger, and so forth. At other times, we may have been influenced by operant conditioning, where we learned to react to some event by either reward or punishment. Many of our habitual reactions, however, were acquired through modeling by peers, parents, teachers, and others.

Later in life, we played a more active part in the formation of our attitudes by habitually pairing our perceptions with evaluative thoughts. Eventually, that process resulted in the continued formation of attitudes—seemingly automatic mental, emotional, and physical reactions.

As long as the formation of our attitudes is based on winning (constructive) thinking—realism, reason, and optimism—we are destined to succeed in life. We find evidence for this throughout human history in virtually all consistent winners. In addition to a winning attitude and winning personality, consistent winners embrace many wholesome goals, including a wholesome philosophy of life—one that is beneficial not just to themselves but to society at large. Real winners are self-made. And that's very good news. It means that you can do the same thing. This book will show you how.

Remember These Points:

- Authentic winners are solution-focused thinkers.
- Authentic winners are both ambitious *and* caring, assertive *and* compassionate.
- Attitudes are habitual predispositions, the result of well-learned and frequently practiced beliefs and mental impressions over a prolonged period.
- Early in life, attitude formation is primarily the outcome of classical conditioning, operant conditioning and modeling.
- Later in life, attitudes continue to be formed mainly by habitually pairing our perceptions with evaluative thoughts.
- Winning thinking is a composite of realism, reason, and optimism.

- Winning thinking is synonymous with constructive thinking and life-enhancing thinking.
- Authentic winners have a winning attitude, a winning personality, and wholesome goals.
- Authentic winners are overcomers; they dominate circumstances, not people!

2

A Winning Attitude Has Three Essential Traits

The Importance of Realism

One of the more troubling developments in modern society is a gradual drifting away from factual into fictional thinking. The movie, music, and publishing industries seem to be in the forefront of leading masses of people into believing all manner of follies.

Perhaps what is missing most in our society—and the world at large—is a desire for truth. Here I am, not speaking about personal truth, but objective reality that is generally accepted *and* independently verified. Opinions, feelings, and beliefs are difficult, if not impossible, to test. Facts, on the other hand, can be tested. And herein lies the power of realistic thinking: the consideration of facts and events as they really are. Realistic thinking is concrete rather than abstract; objective rather than subjective.

Realistic thinking is the kind of thinking that helps us set attainable goals, use blueprints, fly by a compass, have a healthy lifestyle, and do scores of other things that keep us out of the clutches of despair and failure. Realistic thinking shies away from assuming, guessing, and speculating, but simply asks, "Where is the evidence?" If only more people would ask this question, they would not be so easily misled into believing everything they are told. And they also would reject the notion that everything is relative. Objective reality exists independent of our perceptions and thoughts; it is neither relative nor negotiable.

Successful people are nearly always realistic. Consider Helen Keller, who, although extremely rational and positive, was first of all a realist. "I long," wrote Helen, "to accomplish a great and noble task, but it is my chief duty to accomplish small tasks as if they were great and noble." She had a winning attitude, which was squarely based on realism, reason, and optimism. She was scrupulously honest, relied on expert sources of help, had great insight, and was open-minded and flexible. Helen embraced the same basic traits that have been the hallmark of winners throughout history.

The Importance of Reason

While realism focuses on factual information, we find that reason focuses on processing that information. Reason seeks to ensure the validity and reliability of our perceptions and thoughts. *The more reasonable we are, the more likely we will succeed in life.*

Regrettably, most individuals in our society are not very reasonable. A rational person is more the exception than the rule and it is therefore no surprise that about 75-85 percent of our physical and emotional problems are the outcome of self-defeating lifestyles. Most of the problems in our society—whether physical, mental, emotional, relational or social—are primarily the result of unrealistic and irrational thinking. I have discussed this at length in *The Renewed Mind* (1999), *The Consistent Overcomer* (2000) and *The Genesis Wellness Diet* (2007), and will not go into detail here.

Five Helpful Rules for Rational Thinking

There are five very helpful rules for rational thinking I once learned from my favorite teacher, Dr. Maxie C. Maultsby, MD. When three of the following rules are applicable (the first one is not negotiable!), then our thinking is most likely rational:

1. It is objective (factual).
2. It protects our life or health.
3. It helps us to achieve our goals.
4. It helps us to feel calm or happy.
5. It keeps us out of significant conflict.

There are many immediately useful benefits that can be obtained from this simple but highly effective system. For example, you can challenge some of the thinking errors and misbeliefs that may prevent you from having a happier and healthier life. You can do this all the more successfully once you realize that you create your emotions by your thoughts. Our emotional life is mainly a reflection of our thought-life. If you want positive feelings, you first need positive thoughts. "A man," said Ralph Waldo Emerson (1803-1882), "is what he thinks about all day long." Since your mind controls your brain, you can have tremendous control over your thoughts and emotions.

Dr. Maxie C. Maultsby, MD, (1984) holds that while the left hemisphere of the brain is forming beliefs, the right hemisphere is busily engaged in forming attitudes. Maultsby believes that "attitudes are wordless, and therefore unspoken, superconscious forms of beliefs. And [that] beliefs are the spoken or conscious form of attitudes." In whatever way we look at this subject, one thing is clear: *winning or losing in life is more a matter of our attitudes than anything else.* They literally propel us through life and bring us toward our destiny. Happily, we have a choice in the matter. If we want to be consistent winners, we need only to carefully select, and wholeheartedly embrace, life-enhancing thoughts and beliefs.

Nearly everything we do is influenced by our thoughts and beliefs. "Death and life," the book of Proverbs reminds us, "are in the power of the tongue." A more recent point of view was expressed by the Stoic philosophers. "The happiness of your life," wrote Marcus Aurelius, "depends upon the quality of your thoughts." Count Leo Tolstoy (1828-1910), the famous Russian author, also agreed with these sentiments when he said that happiness does not depend on outward things but on the way we see them. And William James, the founder of American psychology, was very excited around the turn of the twentieth century when he discovered that human beings can alter the course of their lives by altering their attitudes.

The power of attitudes really is quite formidable. We can see its negative results in the confusion, crime, misery, turmoil, or violence that results when people are in the grip of destructive attitudes.

And we can see its positive results in the law-abiding behavior and other aspects of societal excellence found in those who have life-enhancing attitudes. A winning attitude is very important if we want to stay alive as happily and successfully as possible. It is a good thing that winning in life does not depend so much on heredity, gender, race, or occupation, as it does on how we think. And how we think is largely a matter of choice.

The Importance of Optimism

In this book, I will somewhat arbitrarily use optimism rather than *positivism* as the third building block of a winning attitude. I know there are subtle differences between the two, but these are of little consequence here. Both positivism and optimism deal with cheerful, confident, and hopeful expectations. I think we can safely use either positive thinking or optimistic thinking as the third building block of a winning attitude.

Of course, it is also possible, and often preferable, to speak of faith as the third building block of a winning attitude (as in truth, reason, and faith). Here, however, we need to more carefully define our terms. While positive thinking is related to faith, it is not identical with it. Faith, as I have explained in *The Renewed Mind* (1999) and *The Consistent Overcomer* (2000), is a gift from God, but positive thinking (optimism) is a learned mental ability—an acquired skill. One that is crucially important, however, for happiness, wellness, and success in life.

There are some who believe realistic and rational thinking are sufficient for a happy and healthy life, but I've failed to find any evidence for this in my own life, or in the lives of the individuals that I've counseled over the past forty years. Optimism is just as essential for a winning attitude, or healthy lifestyle, as realism and reason. Please watch closely the sequence in which these are used. It can be self-defeating to embrace optimism prior to having made a realistic and rational assessment of the situation you are dealing with. Blind optimism can be just as destructive as blind faith. It can literally ruin your life, or the lives of others.

Winners may reach for the stars, but only with their feet planted on solid ground, or—in more modern terminology—while seated securely in a well-supplied space capsule. If they are optimistic that they will reach their goals, they have reason to be optimistic. Blind optimism, on the other hand, is found in such things as gambling, speculating, ignoring safe-driving rules or health-hazard warnings. There is no power in positive thinking unless it's an integral part of constructive thinking. Positive thinking by itself may not deliver anything but disappointment or worse.

Dr. Orison Swett Marden, MD, (1896) tells us that the self-made and optimistic millionaires and billionaires of the nineteenth century were only successful because they had a lot more than positive thinking going for them. They were effective and efficient hard workers. Chance didn't have anything to do with their success. Their achievements were the outcome of realistic discernment and rational decisions, followed by focused effort and boldly taken positive actions. In short, every one of the movers and shakers of the nineteenth century—such as Edison, Bell, Ford, and Rockefeller— were constructive thinkers. Positive thinking was only one part of their approach to lasting success.

Optimism Is a Choice

One way to break the negative self-talk habit is to will yourself to focus above and beyond unpleasant facts or events in your life. It is a determined choice; a decision we make or a mandate that we place on ourselves. A switch from negative thinking to positive thinking always involves effort and may take a number of tries, but sooner or later, you will succeed. In fact, you cannot fail. It was Victor Marie Hugo (1802-1885) who reminded us that above the cloud with its shadow is the star with its light. Negativism, like darkness, has no choice but to eventually succumb to light. We are wise to heed the Chinese proverb that urges us not to curse the darkness but to light a candle. In other words, don't dwell on the problem, but focus on the solution.

Candle lighting is what most of the famous overcomers had to do more than once in their struggle for success. Consider Graham Bell, Christy Brown, Winston Churchill, Charles Dickens, Joni Eareckson Tada, Benjamin Franklin, Agnes Hancock, Helen Keller, Martin Luther King Jr., Abraham Lincoln, Phillippe Pinel, Corrie ten Boom, Mother Teresa, George Peabody, George Washington, and so many others. All of them got up one more time, every time, in the pursuit of their wholesome goals. The candles they lit were candles of realism, reason, and optimism.

Optimism was also the very elixir that helped the Wright brothers persevere until they had their flying machine into the air. It is what helped Edison not to give up until he finally had a workable glass bulb that could bring light into the darkest corner. And optimism is what helped Graham Bell to develop his telephone and bring the people of the world closer together than ever imagined possible.

Optimism is also that special elixir that stirs us into positive action in a world where forces of darkness are trying to sow seeds of terror into the hearts of people everywhere. Those with a strong religious faith and true spiritual persuasion, however, cannot be frightened. They know that death—the king of terror—has already been conquered. And so with determined optimism, but especially faith, we find that those who have a winning attitude are unbeatable. They will get up one more time, every time.

Remember These Points:

- A winning attitude has three *essential traits*: habitual realism, reason and optimism (cf. chapters 24 and 26 on practicing realistic, rational and optimistic thinking!).
- Realistic thinking rejects assuming, guessing, or speculating and focuses on available evidence rather than hearsay and subjective feelings. It embraces objective reality and thus emphasizes the need for accuracy, competence, consistency, discernment, facts, honesty, self-discipline, and other aspects of sound decision making and a truthful life.

- Realistic thinking fosters personal responsibility, such as living within our means and regularly saving or investing whatever we can, regardless of how small the amount.
- Realistic thinking embraces such issues as higher and continued education, the preservation of natural resources, the necessity of a healthy lifestyle in the prevention of illness and the resolution of a worldwide health care crisis.
- Rational thinking is synonymous with reason. It ensures the validity (relative effectiveness) and reliability (trustworthiness) of our thoughts, feelings, and actions.
- Rational thinking fosters sound decision making and promotes a healthy emotional, physical, social, and spiritual life.
- Rational thinking is objective, life-enhancing, goal-achieving, emotionally satisfying and helps prevent or reduce conflict.
- There is no power in positive thinking unless it is an integral part of constructive (winning) thinking.
- Positive thinking is an acquired characteristic; it is different than faith, which is mainly a gift from God.
- It is best to make an optimistic estimate of specific facts and events only *after* we have realistically validated and rationally evaluated them.
- We can alter the direction of our lives by altering our attitudes.
- Winning thinking is a powerful fusion of *realism* with *reason* and *optimism* that furthers personal growth and societal excellence and the achievement of a truly successful and meaningful life.

PART TWO

WINNERS HAVE A WINNING PERSONALITY

PART TWO

3

Winners Are Adaptable

It has been said that variety is the spice of life. But many individuals don't see it that way. They are afraid of change and prefer to keep everything the same. Nothing, however, is static about our existence. Life is a dynamic process. And not only in the physical realm, but also in the emotional, social, and spiritual realm. While spiritual values may not change, our understanding and our experience of these values may change. In order to grow and mature—or even to survive—we continuously must adjust to new and changing realities.

Human Progress Depends on Adaptability

Human beings cannot live very long without the body's ability to adjust to demands made upon it. A balanced physiological state is necessary for wellness and survival, but a balanced psychological state is also necessary. I believe the latter is found through the integration of realism, reason, and optimism. The more realistic, reasonable, and optimistic we are, the better we are prepared to adjust to new challenges.

Human progress has often been slowed by those who were unable and unwilling to adapt themselves to new conditions and opportunities. Many a scholar and inventor has been attacked, ignored, or vilified for some of the most outstanding contributions to science and humanity. Individuals such as *Nicolaus Copernicus* (1473-1543)—who claimed that the sun was at the center of a system in which the earth revolved around it—or *Galileo Galilei* (1564-1642), who was forced to deny the Copernican system. But winners always get up one more time. And even if reason is squelched for a time, it eventually arises victoriously (Gribbin 2007).

Adaptability is necessary if we are going to move forward and succeed in life. This is especially true in the area of interpersonal relationships among members of different philosophical and religious persuasions. Winners take into account that *all* human beings are fallible and imperfect.

The Three Characteristics of Adaptable Individuals

Adaptable individuals are *insightful*. They acknowledge their fallibility and courageously take an in-depth look at what makes them tick. They seek to live by facts and not illusions, by reason and not presumption.

Adaptable individuals are *open-minded*. They are willing to consider the opinions of others and peacefully coexist with them. New and better ways, new methods, new technologies, and new friends are judiciously accepted.

Adaptable individuals are *flexible*. They are able to give or take, lead or follow, speak or listen, and adapt to changes and events that are thrust upon them. Adaptable persons don't have to win every game, debate, or race. Everything does not have to go their way. When circumstances dictate, they can readily lead, willingly follow, or gladly adapt in some other reasonable way.

Remember These Points:

- Individuals who are in the grip of presumptions, close mindedness, and/or inflexibility may find it difficult to adapt to objective reality.
- Life is a dynamic event requiring constant adjustment to changing external and internal conditions.
- Human beings require a balanced physical as well as a balanced psychological state. Without constructive thinking,

it is difficult, if not impossible, to adjust to the many new challenges found in our modern world.

- Adaptability is not a luxury. It is essential for all who wish to succeed, especially in the area of human relationships. It's good to remember that *all* human beings are fallible and imperfect.
- Adaptable individuals are insightful. They recognize that people perish for lack of knowledge and cannot peacefully coexist with others without being open-minded and flexible in human relationships.

4

Winners Are Ageless

Winning in life has a lot more to do with our personality than our age. Just look around and you'll find outstanding leaders who are just starting out on life's journey, and others who have been travelling for a long time. The myth that young persons cannot hold responsible positions is just as misleading as the myth that older persons cannot do so. During the past few decades, we have rediscovered that age has little to do with success in life. Regrettably, there are still parents who believe that their teenage children must be pampered and overprotected, lest their creativity and emotional well-being become stifled.

Of course, it is true that children need the selfless love of their parents. And they need to be protected from the villains in this world who come disguised as sheep but, in reality, are voracious wolves. More than ever, our children need to be closely connected to competent and loving parents. They need to be accepted, respected, listened to, and included in the life of the entire family.

Children, however, don't need to be mollycoddled, allowed to do as they please and turn the family home into chaos. Most teenagers—yes, that includes thirteen-year-olds—are more than ready to share responsibilities around the house, shop, or farm. In fact, not teaching our children at an early age that life is best when they are participants rather than spectators is likely to rob them of a healthy sense of personal worth and future success in life.

I am grateful that I was allowed to help my mother in the house and my father in his bookshops from age eight onward. By the time I was eleven years old—in addition to helping my dad—I had a small collector's stamp business of my own. On Saturdays, when school got out at noon, I would travel several miles through the city to the stamp market in downtown Amsterdam. Here, on a small square in the newspaper district, I'd walk around with a stamp album and a massive outdated French stamp catalog, ready to do business with young and old alike.

At age twelve, I foraged for food in the Dutch countryside with an old bike without tires and brought home sugar beets, potatoes, or anything else that I could find or barter for in those dark days of wartime deprivation. In my late teens, I emigrated to Canada. It was there, and later in the USA, that I quickly learned to appreciate much of what I had learned in my childhood. It saw me through many an unexpected challenge and provided me with many an unexpected opportunity.

Some Famous Americans Who Succeeded Early in Life

Other young people, however, have done a whole lot more with their life experiences than I ever dreamed about. I think it is good to take a brief look at the early lives of a few famous Americans who were definitely not overprotected in their youth, starting with George Washington (Hurlbut 1909).

George Washington was born two hundred years before I first saw daylight. I've got to admit that he was way ahead of me in most other things as well. At age *sixteen*, for example, he was already a successful land surveyor. That job required not only intellectual skills, but also great physical endurance. To do his job, he lived in the forest, travelled over mountains, spent his time with hunters and Indian friends, settled disputes among land owners, kept accurate records of his work, and lived by the golden rule. His teenage years clearly laid the solid foundation for his later success as a great general and as the first president of the United States.

John Paul Jones, America's first navy commander, went to sea as a boy by the name of John Paul at the ripe old age of *thirteen*. Only six years later, at age *nineteen*, he was sailing the North Atlantic as a ship's captain. At age twenty-six, after the death of his brother, he accepted the responsibility for his brother's farm, changed his name to John Paul Jones, and became a farmer. When the war of independence broke out, it was John Paul Jones who insisted that the United States needed ships to fight the British. Imagine this, a young merchant sailor turned farmer would soon be appointed by Congressional Order to lead the United States Navy.

Jones commanded only a handful of small ships while facing an enemy of well-trained professionals with thousands of ships. Nevertheless, he soon became a great naval commander, who fearlessly sailed his ship, *Ranger*, to the shores of England, where he captured several villages. John Paul Jones, perhaps our greatest hero in naval history, fought twenty-three battles, sank scores of ships, and captured several ships to be used in the service of his adopted country.

Benjamin Franklin was only *ten years old* when he started to work in his father's candle shop. And while he enjoyed fishing, swimming, and having fun with his friends, young Ben would spend a great amount of time poring over second-hand books. At age *eleven*, he worked as an apprentice printer at his older brother's printing shop. At age *seventeen*, he left Boston and, after a journey filled with hardships, arrived penniless in Philadelphia where he soon was employed as a printer. Ben Franklin lifted weights, had only bread and milk for breakfast, ate no meat, and drank no alcohol.

Soon, this man, whose formal education ended at age ten, would become a publisher, a scientist who spoke several languages, and founder of a public library in Philadelphia—the first public library in the United States. He invented the lightning rod, received honorary degrees, and became the American ambassador to the French court. Finally, when nearly *ninety years old*, we find him as the president of a society that sought freedom for all people in America. No, it didn't hurt Benjamin Franklin to learn the importance of focused effort and a fine set of values early in life. It greatly benefited him and society at large.

Patrick Henry, of "give me liberty or give me death" fame, was *fifteen years old* when he left school to become a clerk in a country store. At age *sixteen*, his father helped him to have his own store;

but he, along with his brother William, failed in this business. Like most successful persons, Patrick Henry developed a fondness for books—Greek and Roman history in particular. At *age eighteen,* he started married life in a two-room cabin on a small plot of land, but soon failed as a farmer. At age *twenty-one,* he once again tried being a storekeeper, but failed once again.

But Patrick Henry, like all authentic winners who always get up one more time, continued studying history and geography and remained a positive person. At age *twenty-four,* he decided to study law. Within only a few months, he appeared before a law examining board and passed his bar exam. Although inexperienced, poorly trained, and a failure in business and farming, Patrick Henry soon found himself in a Hanover Court, Virginia, successfully arguing that the Episcopal clergy had no right to demand their state pay in tobacco, instead of cash. Focused effort and a winning attitude were the keys to his success!

From that day onward, Patrick Henry was on a steady course. He became a Virginia legislator, commander of the Virginia soldiers, and twice governor of Virginia. Patrick Henry—the great American orator and defender of liberty and a spokesperson for other righteous causes—entered the world of work at age *fifteen.* This early start and hard work prepared him well for his success later in life.

George Peabody, one of the world's great philanthropists, was only *eleven years old* when forced to leave school because of his family's extreme poverty. He became an apprentice in a country store in Danvers, Massachusetts. Five years later, at age *sixteen,* he finished his apprenticeship and was already held in high esteem as an honest and highly competent merchant. George then went to work for his older brother in Newburyport. Not long thereafter, his brother's store was destroyed by fire; and George Peabody moved on to Georgetown, D.C., where, at age *seventeen,* he found work in the dry goods store of an uncle by the name of John Peabody. The latter apparently was a poor businessman who couldn't stay out of debt. George Peabody resigned and started to work for Elisha Riggs, a wholesaler in dry goods. At age *nineteen,* Peabody became the manager of this firm and several months later a full partner.

In his late teens, we find George Peabody travelling to major American cities, doing business for Riggs and Peabody. Not long after that, the firm moved its head office to Baltimore, where, before his *twenty-first* birthday, he became a full partner with Elisha Riggs in a new bank they had cofounded.

The success of Peabody as a powerful merchant and banker in the United States and England is as legendary as his philanthropy. There is no doubt that George Peabody had a winning attitude, winning personality, and wholesome goals.

As a graduate of George Peabody College of Vanderbilt University, I am a grateful beneficiary of the hard work and social conscience of this great American. But the poor people of London were among the greatest beneficiaries of all. George Peabody built decent housing for twenty thousand of London's poorest citizens at a cost of three million dollars—an incredible fortune at that time. Danvers, Massachusetts, the birthplace of George Peabody, has since long been changed to Peabody, Massachusetts. It was one more honor for a man who had already been honored by the queen and prime minister of Great Britain and the United States Congress.

Thomas A. Edison, the world's greatest inventor, attended regular school for two months out of his entire life. When he was only *ten years old,* he had already studied Gibbon's *History of the Rise and Fall of the Roman Empire,* Burton's *Anatomy of Melancholy,* the *Dictionary of Sciences,* and many other scholarly books. Thomas Edison—although at first home-schooled by his mother, a teacher in Port Huron, Michigan—was primarily a self-taught person. At age twelve, he found employment as a railroad newsboy, selling paper, pencils, and books to railway passengers. The more beneficial part of this job was that he could spend his free time in the baggage car, reading books and performing experiments.

Whenever he had a layover in Detroit, young Edison would hasten to the Detroit Free Library where he devoured as many books as he possibly could in the allotted time. At age *fourteen,* his employer awarded him the exclusive rights to a section of the railroad between Port Huron and Detroit, and it didn't take long before Edison hired several boys to help him sell newspapers. At age *fifteen*, he bought some old typesetting equipment from the Detroit Free Press and, together with his young helpers, was soon at work in the baggage car, typesetting and printing a small newspaper *The Grand Trunk Herald*. These early experiences of assertiveness, focused effort, and a winning attitude in Edison's life greatly contributed to the incredible success he had later in life as the world's foremost inventor.

As we turn our gaze away from young Edison, Peabody, Henry, Franklin, Jones, and Washington and take a quick glance at our modern teenagers, we find all too many in trouble with substance abuse, laziness, greed, egotism, procrastination, and boredom. In order to escape the emptiness of their lives and the emotional turmoil of insecurity, instability, and uncertainty, they often seek solace in destructive music or degenerate games and television shows that all too often seemed to have been contrived by disturbed minds.

There are many other reasons why young people are often on self-defeating or self-destructive life tracks. High on the list we find absence of good parental guidance and other good role models, lack of a decent education, learned helplessness, weakness of mind (and body) fostered by junk food, and the list goes on. The good news is that most of this damage can be undone once we conclude that "enough is enough" and begin to explore the many self-development possibilities that are available throughout this country. And there are also many very good role models and success stories that we can turn to. Let me share just one such story from *The Detroit News*, June 7, 2008.

This inspiring story, by Charlie LeDuff, concerns a thirteen-year-old girl by the name of Keiara Bell, who lives amid abject poverty in a destitute and dangerous section of the city of Detroit. However, none of this has apparently prevented her parents from beautifully raising Keiara and her siblings. Living in an economically and socially impoverished neighborhood did not stop Keiara from becoming an authentic winner, finding herself featured on the front page of *The Wallstreet Journal*, being featured in *The Detroit News*, appearing

31

in a video at detnews.com, and making a guest appearance on CBS's *The Early Show*.

What's all the fuss about this bright and engaging girl? I think it's rather simple: Keiara, although very young, is an authentic winner, who recently revealed such winning traits as assertiveness and courage—not to mention ethical standards—when she bravely expressed her heartfelt disapproval of a city council woman's remarks about the Detroit City council president, by telling her, "You're an adult. You have to know your boundaries." But there's a lot more to this story. It reminds us that light is stronger than darkness and that the "sixteen hours a week she spends in church with her family" are not spend in vain.

Keiara Bell, however, is by no means an average American child. Here is a girl who—in modern America—cannot even bring a school book home to study because the school does not have enough books to go around. A school where children must be subjected to indignities such as being patted down before passing through a metal detector. Here's a girl who gladly helps her poor and ailing father sell candy and chips from the trunk of an old car to augment his meager income. A girl quoted as saying, "I'm not ashamed of my family . . . we persevere, and what we have we share." Here is a courageous, solution-focused young girl who not only has a great dream, but who also works hard to make that dream come true. She has already been accepted into a fine public high school and eventually plans to go to college and become a defense attorney. I don't have the slightest doubt that she is destined to succeed in life.

To remove all doubts about the achievements of young people, read *Guinness World Records 2009*. Here you'll find the names of more than a dozen sport champions and Olympic gold medalists, ages thirteen to seventeen, including Marjorie Gestring (USA), Olympic gold medalist at age thireen; and Charlotte Dod (UK), Wimbledon ladies singes tennis champion at age fifteen. On the academic side, you will meet Alia Sabur (USA), who in 2008, at age eighteen, became a full-time faculty professor in technology at Konkuk University, Seoul, South Korea. In 2008, we also find

Mark Zuckerberg (USA), CEO of Facebook, who at age twenty-three already had a net worth of $1.5 billion. In these twenty-first-century achievers, we find similar characteristics as in those of past centuries: commitment, diligence, discipline, focused effort, goal setting, perseverance, and other winning traits!

Success Has No Age Limits

Happily, anyone who can understand this book can turn his or her life around. Also, let's not forget that we have scores of young people who are setting great examples for all to follow. Young men and women who have embraced the importance of accountability, dependability, discipline, and effort.

Before closing this chapter, I would like to say a few words about older winners who can be found throughout society. Take Stanley Kunitz, who several years ago became the U.S. poet laureate. It's no small achievement to be crowned the poet laureate of this country, and especially if you can do this at age *ninety-five*! Stanley Kunitz was quite active even in his "younger" years. For example, when he was only *eighty-seven*, he signed several book contracts, and at age *ninety*, he won the National Book Award.

Stanley Kunitz, however, is not some rarity. There are millions of individuals who are happily and successfully at work in their *eighties* and *nineties*. Like my friend Martin Siegrist, who was still farming at age *ninety-two* and enjoyed every minute of it. American icon, Art Linkletter—entertainer, businessman, humanitarian—is another example of a man who enjoys staying involved. At age *ninety*, he travelled some two hundred thousand miles a year, staying in touch with the world of work and furthering social relationships. It is good to see that not only can many people live longer, but they can also live better! But never without winning thinking!

Many years ago, as a foreign student in Germany, I was sharing a class with a gentleman who was in his *sixties*. In those days, I thought that was really a big thing. I was duly impressed and inspired by it. But nowadays, this would not be a newsworthy event. It's not uncommon to find older students in colleges and universities or people in their *seventies* and *eighties* attending seminars for continuing education units (CEUs) and actively participating in professional conferences.

Several years ago, a fellow Michigander completed her doctoral degree at Michigan State University at age *eighty-six*. Yes, this is a great state! It's the same state where we had a woman in her *eighties* still working as a dental assistant and where many individuals happily and safely drive their own cars well into their *nineties*. Several lived right here in my own town, including then *ninety-six-year-old* Blanche Wagner, who assisted those in need by chauffeuring them around.

At Jim's barbershop, one day, I had a nice talk with then *eighty-year-old* Adrian Perkins, from a town nearby. It wasn't long before the conversation switched from his love for horses to the weather and flying airplanes. Adrian said he just wasn't sure if he would be allowed to take his flying lesson that day because of the gusting winds. But he said he wanted to fly and would go to his flight school—just in case they might let him fly. Listening to Adrian, I couldn't help but wonder how many individuals were staying home that day because the weather was too bad to go out for a haircut.

Adrian Perkins, however, obviously thought it was a great day for getting a haircut as well as for taking to the skies. He reminded me that attitude often determines altitude, and he brought back memories of the pleasant conversations I had years ago with the late Dr. Ormond Barstow of Midland, Michigan. This gentle winner had also taken to the skies when he was already in his *eighties*. And although these two men had different backgrounds, they clearly shared with all other winners—regardless of age—not only a desire for challenging and exciting undertakings, but also a deeply felt sense of contentment and joyfulness. I think Oscar Wilde was right when he said that nothing ages like happiness.

If Adrian Perkins's outlook on life is not enough to get you off the couch and roll up your sleeves, you may consider Cuban musician Francisco Segundo who at age *ninety-four* was still writing music, playing his guitar, singing songs, and staying perfectly in tune with younger generations. But if you're in need of a little more divine inspiration, I suggest you take a look at the Reverend Schreiber. This gentleman attended seminary in his *nineties* and was ordained a minister in the year 2000 at age *ninety-five*. A year later, at age *ninety-six*, as guest chaplain, he vigorously addressed the U.S. house of Congress.

Early Retirement May Be Hazardous to Your Health

Some policy makers believe that early retirement is a good and necessary thing. But I wholeheartedly disagree with them. Not only is our economy negatively impacted by early retirement, but I also think that many individuals, and men especially, are endangered by early retirement. Out of the workforce, separated from companions and friends, no longer intellectually or physically challenged, and ill-prepared for enjoyable or worthwhile postretirement activities, men often feel unnecessary and unwanted. Women, on the other hand, with more varied interests and solid social repertoires, are usually in a better position when they retire early in life.

The evidence is stacking up that many individuals retire too early from the world of work. Others, far worse, just seem to retire from life. They stop being active participants in their communities and shrink from social activities. And some quit fighting for happiness, success, and wellness at the very time that others are just beginning that fight.

Like Dr. Walker, of Norwalk Juicer fame, who, when very ill around age sixty, took up the fight and juiced his way back to health and a joyful life. I understand that he wrote his last book at age *115* and died at age *119*. Please don't fall for the lie that you can't have a healthier and longer life. You have the power to shorten it with an unhealthy lifestyle and you also have the power to lengthen it with a healthy one. The very least, of course, is to be a happy sailor while you're still on board—for a short or long trip. Why not have a purposeful life?

It is best to let go of the myth that young people cannot make wise decisions or hold responsible positions. And it is also time to let go of the myth that life is supposed to be over for those who reach the golden age of three score and ten. As a self-fulfilling prophecy, this could be true, but in reality, it's plain humbug. Whether young or old, you can decide to be a winner and have a solution-focused life.

Remember These Points:

- Winning in life has very little to do with age.
- Young and old, more often than not, are quite capable of acquiring a winning attitude, healthy personality, and wholesome goals.
- There are many individuals who—with diligent study, focused effort, and perseverance—are already successful in their teens.
- Many people find new careers or make major contributions well into their eighties and nineties.
- Poor health and other obstacles must never have the final word regarding success in either young or old.

5

Winners Are Altruistic

Authentic Winners Care for Others

Authentic winners usually don't see themselves as successful unless they are also helping others to succeed in life. Winners look above and beyond themselves and will fight for a good cause. A good example of an authentic winner can be found in the person of Anne Sullivan Macy. This incredibly intelligent, courageous, and dedicated young woman opened wide the doors of life to Helen Keller, a woman of equal standing.

How fitting that half-blind little Anne Sullivan—abandoned, abused, deprived, and one of America's poorest children—should grow up to rescue blind and deaf Helen Keller from a dark and silent world of despair. And to ultimately thrust her into a fullness of life and light that is rarely attained even by those without any serious physical or other challenges.

Anne Sullivan and Helen Keller are undeniably among the greatest overcomers in world history. And it is therefore no surprise that *The Baltimore News*, in glowing terms, once wrote, "To our mind, no record of bravery in war or fortitude in exploration or adventure speaks more eloquently of the power of human will or human courage in their struggle against adverse fate than does the silent work of these two women" (Lash 1980).

Winners know that it is not the possessions they have or leave behind that count, but rather the good they have done with their lives. It is not having possessions, but sharing ourselves and our possessions with others we meet at the colorful crossroads of our lives that brings contentment!

There is no abundant life without selfless love, and there is no success unless it is shared with others. Selfish ambition is a meaningless pursuit and waste of time. It is a wise person, indeed, who embraces altruism and selfless love as a way of life rather than a passing fancy.

Authentic Winners Have Selfless Love

It is increasingly recognized that leadership involves, among other things, responsibility and love for others. I have for some time tried to introduce the concept of love literacy into the workplace via books (Brandt 2003) and seminars. There is simply no question that love is by far "the more excellent way," but this is only slowly being recognized and accepted in the world of work. Nevertheless, many individuals are increasingly beginning to understand that we cannot have either personal or societal excellence without selfless love for others.

As we look at real winners from the dawn of recorded history to the present time, we find that most of them are altruistic individuals. They embrace such values as goodness, justice, and righteousness and seek to help and not to hurt. Focus for a moment on such individuals as Anne Sullivan, Helen Keller, Florence Nightingale, Mother Teresa, Abraham Lincoln, George Peabody, Albert Schweitzer, Thomas Edison, or Graham Bell and you'll find altruistic men and women.

If realism, reason, and optimism are indeed the foundational traits of a winning attitude and success in life, where does selfless love fit into the scheme of things? *Love is simply a logical and inevitable outcome of sound reason* (cf. epilogue). *Love is the central dynamic for a happy life and is essential for the mental, emotional, physical, social, and spiritual wellness of every human being.* The absence of selfless love, and hence of happiness, can nearly always be traced to unhealthy personality styles.

The good news is that with due diligence we can acquire a healthy personality that includes such traits as benevolence, kindness, and selflessness. To be a leader, or a winner, we must love (accept, respect, and understand) others. It is essential for personal and societal excellence.

Love Is the Greatest Power on Earth

It may seem strange that I am including altruism and love as character traits of winners. But in reality, they are the most important of all the traits we find in authentic winners. A common, but mistaken, concept of winners is to see them as selfish and combative. These characteristics are not congruent with affection, compassion, selflessness, and similar traits that we associate with a loving person.

Winners are often perceived as manipulative and shrewd or superior to others. Mind you, it's not strange that winners are perceived in this way. After all, many influential people see themselves in this manner. Some have narcissistic personalities and truly believe they are superior and entitled to favoritism. Many in our society have been seduced into believing that might makes right.

The reason why real winners are altruistic is rather simple. As explained earlier, *love is an expression and a reflection of sound reason.* Many winners, however, love others for its intrinsic value. It's wholesome. It's right. It makes sense. It is God's will. Many winners, however, have discovered that *love is truly the greatest power on earth.* They learned that love is indispensable for emotional, mental, physical, social, and spiritual well-being. And although some individuals wish to dispute it, there is no meaningful existence without love (Gordon 1903; Brandt 2003).

Remember These Points:

- The three *primary* winning traits—realism, reason, and optimism—are absolutely necessary to be a winner in life.
- The more *secondary* winning traits a person has, the greater the chances for permanent success in life.
- Altruism—benevolence—is a very important aspect of selfless love.

- Authentic winners see themselves as successful only if they also help others to succeed.
- Winners who are famous for their altruism include Abraham Lincoln, Helen Keller, Anne Sullivan Macy, Florence Nightingale, Corrie Ten Boom, Mother Teresa, Albert Schweitzer, and George Peabody.
- Egotism is increasingly seen as a handicap and a dangerous trait for managers in the world of work.
- Selfless love is the central dynamic for meaning and purpose in life; a logical outcome of applied reason.
- Love literacy is slowly being accepted as a necessary aspect of leadership in the world of work.
- Love is both an expression and reflection of sound reason.
- Love is, unquestionably, the greatest healing power on earth.

6

Winners Are Assertive

Stop for a moment and reflect on the number of winners you know who are not assertive. It is not difficult to come up with the names of a few nonassertive persons who are successful in their careers and perhaps in other areas of their lives. As a rule, however, we find that winners are assertive individuals.

Of course, not all winners have the same number of winning traits. The only three traits that are essential for a winning attitude are realism, reason, and optimism. The more secondary winning traits we have, however, is all the better for lasting success.

Winners Dare to Be Themselves

One of the more helpful winning traits is assertiveness: the ability and willingness to stand up for oneself. Asserting yourself means that you are not afraid or ashamed to let others know what your opinion or position is on a given subject. It may also mean that you are willing to defend your beliefs, standards, morals, or values and are unwilling to have people walk over you. On the other hand, it can also mean that you want others to know that you are capable of standing on your own feet and can do most things in life without an overreliance on others.

It is, of course, not always easy to assert oneself. There are many powerful forces that will oppose you in this matter. Cult leaders, for example, are well-known for their desire to have complete control over their followers. They are intolerant of those who stand up for themselves or defend any belief that contradicts them. At a far less

41

severe level, we find that some corporations, institutions, schools, and other organizations may claim the right to defend their position, yet refuse to listen to, or stifle, the opinions of their employees, members, students, and so forth.

The same thing is often found in other relationships. For example, narcissistic persons will not tolerate anything that hints of independence in their handpicked admiring spouses. The latter are expected to take orders and have no opinions. It is difficult enough for a dependent or codependent person to assert him or herself under the best of circumstances, but it is a herculean task when dealing with a narcissistic spouse. Yet the answer to having happier and healthier relationships must include not only less egotism in the controlling person, but more assertiveness in the dependent one (Brandt 2003).

Fearful People Develop Unhealthy Personality Styles

To assert yourself in everyday life means that you are willing to express your thoughts, beliefs, and feelings in a free and honest manner. Winners embrace honesty with the same passion that they embrace other aspects of assertiveness that are important for success in life and physical and emotional wellness. Individuals who are afraid to express themselves often develop unhealthy personalities, where outwardly they act agreeable, but inwardly they are quite disagreeable.

Assertiveness is a very rational trait. Assertive persons don't speak up to get even or to hurt someone. They merely want to protect themselves, correct injustices, heal divisiveness, and protect hurting or needy persons. Assertiveness is also a very realistic and positive trait that seeks to prevent as well as solve problems and wrongs.

Assertiveness versus Aggressiveness

It is important to make a distinction between assertiveness—a constructive defense of oneself or others on behalf of liberty, justice, and so forth—and aggressiveness (a destructive attack on others that seeks to accuse, blame, divide, or humiliate). Assertiveness in interpersonal relations is healthy, but aggressiveness is not. In our society we find many individuals with antisocial personality styles who are outwardly very charming but inwardly very aggressive. When sufficiently frustrated, they'll toss their charms by the wayside and unleash their hidden aggressiveness. This, of course, is not the way to make friends and influence people. Aggressiveness always backfires!

Assertive individuals, however, are likely to succeed in getting the results they hope to get. They are in a win-win position. Even if they don't get their way, they have the satisfaction of being true to themselves. Being part of the solution rather than the problem, they reap immediate benefits for their physical, emotional, and spiritual health. Suppressing our displeasure, on the other hand, about an important issue may lead to health problems and many other difficulties.

It is not easy to switch from being a nonassertive person to being an assertive one. There are two obvious reasons for this. It may feel phony to you, for it goes against your well-learned behavior. Additionally, you may encounter much opposition from your boss, coworkers, friends, and children, but especially your spouse. Your newfound assertiveness may, at first, go over like a "lead balloon."

Remember These Points:

- Assertiveness—the ability and willingness to stand up for oneself—is important for happiness and success in life.
- Assertive persons are not afraid of rejection or ashamed of failures and mistakes that are part of being fallible and imperfect.
- Assertiveness is necessary to prevent manipulation, intimidation, and domination by cult leaders and other personality-disordered persons.
- Assertive individuals are outwardly and inwardly far more congruent than those who are avoidant and fearful.

- Assertiveness can provide some protection against injustices, heal divisiveness, and help resolve other interpersonal challenges.
- Controlling persons and cult leaders are intolerant of assertive individuals.
- Nonassertive individuals often develop unhealthy personality styles.
- Nonassertive individuals who eventually dare to be themselves are likely to encounter much opposition from their immediate environment.
- Nonassertiveness contributes to burnout among those who are caught up in the rat race of work for the sake of work or servitude for the sake of peace.
- Assertiveness is important for happiness, wellness, and success in all areas of life, whether in the world of work, at home, or elsewhere.

7

Winners Are Committed

W inners are committed to many wholesome endeavors. For example, they will readily support a worthy cause, stick to the rules of a contract, and uphold ethical standards of behavior. But within the context of this book, I am thinking more about the stick-to-it commitment of a winning attitude that we find in winners. They are full-time, solution-focused participators who are always ready to lead the way. In order to achieve their wholesome goals, they deliberately do whatever needs to be done.

Winners burn bridges behind them, look to the future, stay focused on goals, and remain loyal to a just cause; they are committed to succeed. It is not possible to have the energy, stamina, and will to succeed, unless we are fully persuaded to reach some high ideal or fight for some noble cause. Winners know they must stand for something or be in danger of falling for anything. Winston Churchill was acutely aware of the need to be victorious over the powers of darkness his nation faced during World War II. "Victory at all costs," he cried out, "victory in spite of terror, victory however long and hard the road may be; for without victory there is no survival."

Commitment Requires Self-Discipline

Many years ago I volunteered my services at a substance abuse center to conduct group therapy for a few hours a week. I was also busy with other projects and had not agreed to come in on a regular basis, but on an "I'll try to make it" basis. Most weeks, I would show up, but there were times that I did not.

One day, one of my friends at the center asked if I would be back again next week. I gave my standard reply, "I'll try to be here, Arney." Instead of a slap on the back for volunteering, I received a lecture. "Don't come back, Frans, unless you can commit yourself to this program. We have enough clients who are 'trying' to do things. We are not looking for therapists who 'try' to do something, but for those who 'do' something. Will you be here next week, or won't you? Tell me now." I told him, "Yes." Guess what, I never again missed a meeting once I had fully committed myself to helping my friends and their clients.

Success is not a spectator sport, nor is it achieved by hoping or wishing, but only by focused effort and hard work. Commit yourself to harnessing your will and rise above the mediocre and mundane if you want a purposeful and successful life. Winners succeed because they are persuaded there is no other acceptable choice. "Most powerful," wrote Seneca, "is he who has himself in his own power." I think that's what commitment is really all about.

Remember These Points:

- Authentic winners support worthy causes, abide by the rules of a contract, and support the ethical standards of behavior of a civilized society.
- Winners burn their bridges, stay focused on goals, and persevere in spite of challenges or hardships.
- Commitment requires firm decisions that are adhered to, even if at times this is difficult or unpleasant.
- Commitment involves fully surrendering oneself to agreed upon personal, social, and/or spiritual goals and standards.
- Commitment requires active participation and a willingness to lead or follow.

- Winners are committed to defend and protect the well-being of those placed in their care, whether at home, school, or the workplace.
- Winners are committed to rise above the mediocre and mundane.
- Commitment is hard work that requires self-control, self-denial, and perseverance.

8

Winners Are Competent

In this book, we are talking about authentic winners; genuine individuals with a winning attitude based on realism, reason, and optimism. However, there are lots of wonderful people who cannot do this because of organic brain impairment or some other reason. These individuals, however, are often winners in their own right. Just think about their achievements in the Special Olympics and in day-to-day life. About thirty-five years ago, I had an opportunity to deliver some Christmas gifts to patients in a mental hospital in North Dakota. I had looked forward to this event, thinking it would be nice to bless some of the young people in that institution. As things turned out, however, I was the one who was blessed the most.

I'll never forget how great it felt to be around so many fantastic young people, in spite of Down syndrome and other impairments. The thought struck me that surely this is what angels must look like in heaven. I was thoroughly convinced that these young people, and so many in similar circumstances, are real winners. They are in possession of some mysterious grace and, paradoxically, are so often ahead of many who don't have these challenges. At that institution, I found people with an honest charm. Young and old alike were blessed with a beguiling innocence, eyes that sparkled, faces that glowed, and smiles sometimes more alluring than Mona Lisa's.

Competent Individuals Have High Ideals

Besides mentioning the importance of competence in the life of authentic winners, I need to say something about the many people who, to no fault of their own, are not in a position to fully take care of themselves. I want to make it clear that I don't see them—or anyone else for that matter—as inferior to other people. All human beings are fundamentally alike. There are no superior or inferior people, only fallible ones. Having said this, we must not lose sight of the fact that fallible people may do bad things or good things. A fallible person can be a saint or sinner and can perform in an inferior or superior way. Winners, however, always do their very best to be as competent as possible in their chosen work or calling.

Winners want to be competent because they know that competence and focused effort are essential if they are going to succeed in the world of work or any other aspect of life. Authentic winners accept personal responsibility, have a solution-focused orientation, and are committed to life-enhancing and goal-achieving endeavors. They know that the way in which they habitually think determines the way in which they habitually live.

Winners seek to be fully competent because they want to be part of the solution and not part of the problem. They know that societal excellence is only possible with multiplied personal excellence. Every well-known authentic winner is a hardworking, self-made individual. Their success in life is not based on some inheritance, connections, or so-called good luck, but on focused effort and hard work.

Real winners are competent because they are determined, disciplined, industrious, and persevering visionaries. In this country, we have scores of individuals who are not unlike some of the famous individuals I mention in this book. We have numerous individuals who grow up poor, yet rise above the most challenging circumstances. Individuals who continue to prove that there is very little that cannot be accomplished by those who are deliberately dedicated to a cause that is greater than themselves.

Remember These Points:

- Not everyone has the same window of opportunity to be fully competent.

- Competence within the context of this book refers to being adequately trained and sufficiently qualified for a particular endeavor in the world of work or elsewhere.
- Authentic winners or not, there are no inferior or superior people. All human beings remain fallible and imperfect.
- Winners seek to be as competent as is humanly possible.
- Competence and focused effort are necessary for happiness, success, and wellness in life.
- There is little that cannot be accomplished by those who are sufficiently skilled and dedicated to a task at hand.

9

Winners Are Consistent

It is a great tragedy whenever lack of consistency is found in individuals who are somehow in leadership positions. It is not uncommon to find those who, for the sake of political correctness or for expediency, will contradict not only their own beliefs, but also the very teachings of the group, organization, or even the religion they claim to embrace or represent.

Inconsistency Leads to Failure

Needless to say, if there is a lack of consistency among those who are in leadership positions, it will also be reflected in the behavior of their followers. Inconsistent supervisors have an inconsistent workforce, inconsistent parents have inconsistent children, and inconsistent preachers have an inconsistent congregation. The harm that is being done by those who operate from shifting sand is quite considerable. In the workplace, for example, it may result in absenteeism, accidents, discontent, illness, lowered productivity, poor quality of work, sabotage, and even violence. In the home, inconsistency may lead to anger, anxiety, depression, confusion, conduct disorders, oppositional behavior, substance abuse, and many other problems. And when it comes to inconsistency among religious leaders, the fallout is often so serious that the wounds inflicted on the faithful are often difficult to heal. When preachers or teachers are exposed as frauds, or merely as hirelings who say one thing but do another, the emotional and spiritual wounds inflicted on the faithful are usually deep and very long lasting.

It goes without saying that inconsistent people—those who don't say what they mean or mean what they say or talk the talk but don't walk the walk—are outside the winner's circle. Some time ago, I heard Dr. Ravvi Zacharias say that in a survey conducted in Canada, the number one desire among Canada's youth was to find someone they can believe in. But that someone, of course, *is* here. Before we place our trust in people, it is best to first discover the one sure epitome of love, coherence, and solidarity: God.

This does not mean that there are no individuals on the face of the earth that we can believe in. There have always been those who—although fallible—have proven to be consistent winners. To the best of my knowledge, these are, more often than not, those who themselves had earlier placed their trust in the God of the Ten Commandments. A God of principles, standards, and values. I am thinking of individuals such as Dietrich Bonhoeffer, who was executed in 1945 by the Nazis, precisely because he was a man of principle, a man of his word, a person we can believe in.

And there are scores of individuals who, throughout history and to this very day, have neither faltered nor changed their principles for money, self-glorification, or political correctness. Several of these individuals are mentioned in various places throughout this book—Albert Schweitzer, George Peabody, Corrie Ten Boom, Mother Teresa, G. K. Chesterton, and so many others. Youth of Canada, take heart!

What we need, of course, is discernment. We must open our eyes and ears and refuse to be distracted by the clatter of empty noisemakers or the glitter of their tinsel and fluff. Listen closely. There are no wishy-washy winners. Inconsistent individuals who will do whatever it takes to maintain their fragile egos. And not only at your expense, but also even at the expense of their own "avowed" values. Consistent winners, on the other hand, are quite different. They are congruent, dependable, faithful, generous, harmonious, open, reliable, steady, and trustworthy. Although fallible and imperfect, they are still the kind of people we can believe in. What a wonderful challenge and great example consistent winners present to a world adrift with inconsistent people.

Remember These Points:

- Inconsistent behavior by people in leadership positions tends to breed inconsistent behavior in their charges and followers.
- Inconsistent behavior is often found among greedy and egotistical individuals.
- Inconsistent behavior by those in authority may result in great harm, whether at home, school, church, or the workplace.
- Famous consistent winners include Corrie Ten Boom, Dietrich Bonhoeffer, G. K. Chesterton, George Peabody, Albert Schweitzer, and Mother Teresa.

10

Winners Are Content

Contentment Is a Matter of the Heart

Those who have a winning attitude, winning personality, *and* wholesome goals know that real happiness has nothing to do with fame or power. True happiness is a matter of the heart and involves, first of all, healthy relationships based on love, altruism, honor, and integrity. Even health *and* wealth, by and of themselves, cannot bring lasting happiness. Many individuals are on a futile search for contentment. This is what I said elsewhere:

> Lacking insight into the nature of their predicament, unable to deal with the many stressors around them, and often devoid of a moral or spiritual anchor, millions of individuals are on a futile search. Futile, because they believe that the solution to their problems lies primarily in finding the right kind of partner or some other external factor. Futile, because a lasting solution can only be found in a fundamental and permanent change in our mental, emotional and spiritual orientation. We must rid ourselves of the misconception that we are merely bystanders on the road to happiness, wellness and success. We must rid ourselves of the notion that we are mere pawns being moved across the chessboard of life by powerful external forces. While other individuals and many of life's events may provide various circumstances over which we can make ourselves happy or unhappy, the fact remains that

> most of us, at least in our society, have the final say over
> our emotional wellness. (Brandt 1984, 1999)

Contentment is not the outcome of power and riches or the birthright of the few. Contentment is a choice. A choice, by and large, independent of external events. This fact was proven over and over in our more recent history. After the worst terrorist attacks on American soil, thousands of innocent lives were lost, and thousands of others who had escaped death were seriously traumatized. Others who were also deeply traumatized included the rescuers, and of course, those who had lost a spouse, father, mother, son, daughter, friend, or coworker.

Yet shortly after these indescribably horrible events in New York, Pennsylvania, and at the Pentagon, there were many individuals who—despite having lost someone very dear to them under the cruelest of circumstances—flatly refused to yield to despair, fear, hatred, or other destructive emotive feelings. How could some women who had lost their husbands appear on television, calm and poised, and speak of life rather than death? How could they rally around their grieving children with words of comfort and encouragement and, with great determination, let it be known that no one was going to steal their joy? Who are these individuals? Are they modern Stoics who have trained their minds to obey their every command? I don't think so.

I think that most of these highly resilient individuals were authentic winners long before this awful tragedy took place. Most of them were already poised to face adversities and hardships. These individuals were already determined that nothing on earth—and certainly nothing from hell—could ever steal their faith, zest for life, love for their children, precious memories of loved ones or anything else they held dear.

True contentment doesn't just happen, it's the outcome of a long process involving mind and spirit. Perhaps there are some genetic personality traits that play a part in the deep contentment we find in winners. More important factors, however, are found in those learned behaviors that enable so many individuals to choose their own level of contentment with as little outside interference as humanly possible. But of course, not every individual has the same window of opportunity, and hence, it's not true that happiness is always a choice. Let's have a closer look at this.

Happiness Is Usually a Choice

First of all, a warning. We are living in a time where there is often unconditional acceptance that genetics is the primary player in our happiness and well-being. This is very foolish and leads to apathy and lack of responsibility. In spite of recent developments in the field of genetics, we must come to our senses. All of history shows that most human beings can alter their attitudes and can transform their lives. History proves that human beings can overcome incredible hardships and challenges. We are foolish if we overlook that most people ultimately write their own ticket to happiness. But it's not true that happiness is *always* a choice for everyone. This is what I said in *The Consistent Overcomer.* While happiness is a choice for most individuals (at least in our society), it is completely wrong to say that happiness is always a choice. To choose happiness, we need to have a functioning brain, a certain amount of intellectual ability, education, training, information, and so forth. Millions of individuals with seriously impaired brain chemistry find it very difficult and, at times impossible, to be happy (Brandt 2000).

·Not All Happiness Is the Same

While it is true that most of us can choose our own level of happiness, it is important to remember that happiness may mean one thing to one person and another thing to another person. There may well be thousands of descriptions, definitions, and opinions on the subject of happiness. Since happiness involves perceptions, cognitions, emotions, and behavior, we can see it as a *mental state* (e.g., contentment), an *emotive state* (e.g., pleasure or delight), and/ or a *physical state* (e.g., as in certain biochemical and physiological events). We can summarize this by saying that happiness is a positive mental, emotive, and/or physical event. But there are also other ways to look at happiness.

For example, we can say that authentic happiness is an enduring frame of reference: a mind-set that often transcends challenging circumstances. Happiness, from this point of view, is more a mood than an emotion, more an attitude than a belief, and more an internal disposition than a response to some external event. This kind of happiness is pervasive and colors every aspect of one's life. Happiness as an enduring mood is different than mere fleeting emotional states such as cheerfulness, delight, or gladness. Happiness comes in a variety of degrees; it can be shallow or profound. It is definitely more than some undifferentiated feeling state that exists apart from our value system or the bad and good choices we make. All happiness clearly is not the same.

Winners are alert to the fact that there is false and true happiness. The former consists of the fraudulent happiness found in those who lead corrupt, immoral, or otherwise destructive lives but who present themselves as happy individuals. Certain personality-disordered individuals enjoy false happiness by manipulating, intimidating, and/or dominating others. True happiness, on the other hand, lines up with such values as goodness, kindness, and mercy. It seems that those with authentic happiness are as concerned with others as with themselves. They have a well-developed social conscience and will readily share their time and possessions with those who are less well-off.

Authentic winners focus on wholesome thoughts and beliefs. They have no time for self-blame, other blame, self-pity, or such negative emotive feelings as anger, bitterness, hatred, jealousy, rage, or resentment. Winners are quick to forgive and to move on with life and living. They know that unforgiveness keeps people in chains that prevent them from succeeding in life. They know that harboring resentment is a poison for the whole person: body, mind, and spirit.

Authentic winners are content because they know that the secret of happiness is not found in success that focuses on power, prestige, and privilege. They know that real success focuses on meaning, purpose, values, and other wholesome goals. Contentment is found in doing good for others and doing our very best to leave this world just a tiny bit better than we found it upon our arrival, and that is just one of many things real winners care about.

Remember These Points:

- Contentment is a matter of the heart: a mental disposition of being fully at peace with one's condition in life.
- Contentment is analogous with true happiness; the outcome of many choices over time that involve body, mind, soul, and spirit.
- True happiness involves meaning and purpose and is found in those who embrace such values as a social conscience, reverence for life, and selfless love.
- Not all happiness is the same and not all people have the same window of opportunity for happiness. Yet most people, ultimately, write their own ticket to happiness.

11

Winners Are Cooperative

Winners try to stay clear from events that may lead to significant conflict with their environment. I am talking about the kind of conflict they don't want or are unable to handle. Obviously, not all conflict can be avoided. There will always be difficult individuals that you may need to deal with, including those who intentionally create trouble for you. It would be nice to surround ourselves only with people who have a healthy personality, but this is not always possible. Nevertheless, it is important, and sometimes essential, to get along with some very difficult individuals.

Abraham Lincoln wisely said that we cannot fool all the people all the time, and of course, we wouldn't want to. But it is usually in our best interest to get along even with those who dislike us for one reason or another. It is always best not to criticize these people or to constantly focus on differences. It is far more rational to search for agreements and to do good things even for those who oppose us.

In order to get along with others, it is necessary to be an objective and patient listener and to communicate our thoughts and feelings both verbally and nonverbally. Remember that there are very specific reasons why people want to get along with us. They may do so more out of need than love. Ideal relationships, however, are selfless.

The Most Important Human Need

The secret of getting along with others is not so much found in techniques (although it is important to remember the names, concerns, and interests of others!) as in having a healthy, winning personality, and embracing a constructive philosophy of life. While all individuals have needs, limitations, and strengths, they have only one overriding emotional need: love! It is also important to remember that all people are fallible and imperfect, and that most of them like to stay alive as long as possible and want to feel good emotionally.

But never overlook that the number one need all human beings share is the need to love and be loved. In practical terms, they have a need to be accepted, appreciated, respected, and understood. Of course, affectionate and romantic love is a somewhat different matter as I have described in *How to Get Along With Yourself and Others* (Brandt 2003).

I believe it can safely be said that most people primarily get along with us because we meet one or more of their needs. There are things about us that enable them to feel better about themselves or life in general. Because most of our troubles are the outcome of irrational behavior (75-85 percent of all physical and mental health challenges in this country are due to faulty lifestyles), there is a demand for individuals who have constructive lifestyles. If you have a winning attitude, healthy personality, and *needed* job skills, you are in great demand in the world of work and elsewhere.

You are in demand because of your ability to get along even with those who dislike or oppose you. You also know that your emotions are self-created, and you simply reserve the right to obey the commandment to love your enemies. In order to get along with others, it is imperative to know that no two individuals can experience anything in an identical manner. In the book of Proverbs, we read that "every man's way is right in his own eyes." And that's it! The more we realize that *all* human beings are fallible, the less we upset ourselves over individual differences or opinions.

How to Get Along with Others

In order to have cooperative relationships, it is a good idea to create change conditions. These are simply conditions you create that may induce others to see you in a different light. It's futile to demand that difficult people be different. The only guaranteed event that will happen is that you'll make yourself angry. It is far better to learn what kind of personality style they have (see chapter 24) and to remain objective and dispassionate. If you have a winning attitude and healthy personality, you are able to create change conditions and get along with most people.

Being cooperative does not mean we have to agree with everything that other people believe, say, or do. It is possible to disagree with someone's behavior or philosophy of life, yet have a very cooperative relationship at work or in many other settings. In my own work, I frequently see individuals whose beliefs and behaviors are quite different than mine. Yet as a rule, I have been able to successfully work with them.

Earlier, I mentioned the importance of having some idea of the dominant personality style of those we associate or work with. Later in this book, I mention some unhealthy personality styles within the context of a person's general demeanor. If a person's overall lifestyle is dominated by *unrealistic, irrational,* and/or *negative* perceptions, thoughts, feelings, and/or behaviors, it is quite likely that this person has an unhealthy personality style. To more fully understand the many ramifications of this, you may wish to take a look at *How to Get Along With Yourself and Others* (Brandt 2003).

Remember These Points:

- When dealing with conflict, focus on the issues rather than the person. If at all possible, stay clear from conflict you are unable or unwilling to deal with.
- To form cooperative relationships, it is necessary to be an objective and patient listener, using only appropriate and limited self-disclosure. It must be pertinent to the issues at hand and necessary for a successful agreement or resolution of conflict.
- To get along with others refrain from arguing, blaming or criticizing, harping on differences, or trying to get even.

- Hope, wish, work, and pray for others to get along with you, but never demand this. The latter makes things worse.
- All human beings are fallible. They may truly believe they are right, even if objective reality proves otherwise.
- Virtually, all human beings have a need to love and be loved.

12

Winners Are Courageous

It is difficult to find an authentic winner who is not a courageous person. And I am not only thinking about those who risk their lives for others. I am also thinking of those who freely and unhesitatingly do other gallant things with their lives. For example, Samuel Johnson (1709-1784), that heroic laborer who single-handedly performed the gargantuan task of compiling his famous *Dictionary of the English Language* (1755). Johnson knew a thing or two about quotations, and when he says that courage is the greatest of all virtues, we had better sit up straight and pay close attention.

Courage and Virtue Go Hand in Hand

Other famous individuals, such as C. S. Lewis (1898-1963) and Sir Winston Churchill (1874-1965), also maintained that courage is at the heart of every virtue. How strange that this is not being taught in every classroom of every school in our nation. Two hundred years ago, *Barclays Dictionary* (1812) defined courage as "a braveness of mind, which enables a person to run any risks, undergo any difficulties and confront any dangers, arising from a sense of duty, and a fear of offending him that made us." Regrettably, in our modern dictionaries, you'll look in vain to find a connection between courage and a sense of duty, let alone a fear of offending God. How sad!

In the absence of courage, there is no virtue; and in the absence of virtue, there are no true winners. My definition of a winner includes *the pursuit of wholesome goals*, which is, of course, synonymous with *virtuous goals.* Goals that support the rules of morality—good, just, loving, and merciful rules. As we look at winners such as George Washington (1732-1799)—whose honesty and openness as a youth was legendary and whose courage never faltered—or Abraham Lincoln (1809-1865), who rose from abject poverty and extreme deprivation to a position of trust that was beyond the grasp of the most powerful rulers in the world, we find their courage was intrinsically interwoven with a strong sense of duty to God and all of humanity.

History is filled with overflowing examples of courageous winners, and the best I can do here is to simply mention a few of them. Courageous women like Florence Nightingale, Anne Sullivan, Helen Keller, Corrie ten Boom, Rosa Parks, Marie Curie, and Mother Teresa. Courageous men such as Mahatma Gandhi, Louis Pasteur, Christian Barnard, Nelson Mandella, Jonas Salk, Albert Schweitzer, and Reginald Mitchell—who sacrificed his life to design the Spitfire airplane that saved Britain, and perhaps the world, from defeat during the Battle of Britain in the summer of 1940.

I list the names of these few individuals as a reminder that every true winner is a courageous person—including, of course, the heroic pilots—most of whom died or got wounded during that great battle I've just mentioned. It's important to remind ourselves that the freedom and blessings we enjoy today didn't come about by accident but were paid for by the blood, sweat, and tears of courageous men and women—then and now.

The Many Faces of Courage

Courage comes in many forms and knows neither age, gender, nor race. I have already written about the agelessness of winners in an earlier chapter, but would like to bring this into the context of courage. Marden (1896) mentions that Alexander the Great (356-323 BC) had "conquered the whole known world before dying at thirty-three. Washington was appointed adjutant-general at age nineteen, was sent at twenty-one as an ambassador to treat with the French, and won his first battle as a colonel at twenty-two, and Lafayette was made general of the whole French army at twenty."

Galileo was only eighteen when he discovered the principle of the pendulum, Gladstone was in the British parliament at age twenty-one, Elizabeth Barrett Browning had fully mastered Greek and Latin at age twelve, Robert Browning wrote poetry at age eleven, and Horatio Nelson was a lieutenant in the British navy at age nineteen. On the other side of the coin, we find that the same Gladstone who was in Parliament at age twenty-one was also an outstanding prime minister at age eighty-four. No matter how young or old, it is often *courage* that decides the difference between victory or defeat.

It also takes fortitude and valor to find our personal place or calling in a selfish and restless world. In *The Return of the Prodigal Son*, Henry Nouwen (1992) addresses his spiritual journey from not feeling loved enough by his good but fallible human father to a greater understanding and more intimate relationship with his infallible heavenly Father. When Henry Nouwen's dad flew over from Holland to visit his son in the New World, he told his dad—for the first time in his life—that he loved him and that he was grateful for his father's love. The courage to love those whose love for us may at times fall short, or even be absent altogether, sometimes may seem more difficult than conquering the world.

Courage, as I said earlier, has no age limits. We find incredible courage in young children like Mattie Stepanek, who at age eleven, while battling an incurable illness had such a powerful winning attitude that it lifted the spirits of all who met him or read his inspiring essays and poetry. Here was an eleven-year-old boy who looked death in the face and had a social conscience so strong and a heart so big that he could say it was better for him to have an incurable illness than some baby. Why? Because he believed that he could understand the problem and deal better with it. Here was a young boy, confined to a wheelchair and attached to a bottle of oxygen, who was cheerful, helpful, grateful, friendly, polite, optimistic, and courageous. Mattie (Matthew) Stepanek showed the whole world that courage is indeed the greatest of all virtues and can be found in people of *all* ages!

The courage of those who have major physical challenges is often legendary. Sometimes we learn about their successes in books they have written or that have been written about them, and at other times, we are blessed to know some of them personally. Take Erik Weihenmaier who, at age thirty-two, became the first blind person to reach the summit of the world's most challenging mountain, Mount Everest. But this is not the only mountain Erik has climbed. He has successfully climbed some of the most difficult mountains in Africa, Antarctica, Asia, North America, and South America. He has written an inspiring book, *Touch the Top of the World*, in which he spells out in words—what he has already spelled out in deeds—that *winning is a choice*. A choice that beckons most of us in one way or another.

In addition to having read about the lives of many consistent winners, I've also been blessed to meet many in my professional and personal life. Let me briefly say a few words about two sightless persons that I have had the privilege of knowing. First, there is a sightless girl who used to come to some of my early presentations on self-counseling here in Michigan. She never complained about the challenges that faced her. She always had a smile on her face and a willingness to share her life with others. She actively participated in a program of personal growth. While attending my self-counseling classes, she typed one of my books in braille for other sightless persons. Like so many persons with major challenges, she always looked for ways in which she could help others.

Another sightless person I am privileged to have known is Robert Blair. A gentleman who became blind in the prime of his life, with a large family to take care of and no spouse to help him. Although completely blind, he managed not only to survive economic and family hardships, but also to earn a bachelor's and master's degree and then teach living skills to blind students at Yuma Center for the Blind in Yuma, Arizona. Among the many things that inspire me about him is that he was a peacemaker. A man who looked for the best in everyone he met and who treated them with a helpfulness and kindness that puts many sighted people to shame. There was no complaining, bitterness, jealousy, or selfishness in this gentleman. Here was a man, who, in spite of physical challenges, led an independent life and looked above and beyond himself.

Whether we talk about the courage of Samuel Johnson, the man who single-handedly wrote a famous English dictionary; Abraham Lincoln, who stood for justice and equality; Albert Schweitzer, who reached out to suffering humanity; Henri Nouwen, who tackled a great personal challenge; Harry Ramos, who sacrificed his life at the World Trade Center in New York; Erik Weihenmaier, who climbed to the summit of life itself; or any other true winner—we will find again and again *there is no winning in life without courage.*

I have observed that much of the complaining and whining does not come from people who face real obstacles but from those who have lesser challenges and setbacks. It often comes from those who are spoiled or overprotected and may have never spent a day in the service of their country, done any volunteer work, or had any interest in those who toil for them. While some couples battle over who failed to put the cap on the toothpaste tube, others are fighting real life and death battles to make the world a better and safer place.

Discontented people should take another look at the events of September 11, 2001. There were numerous winners that day, courageous people like the emergency workers, firefighters, police officers, and so many others who stood tall even when the buildings in which they found themselves could no longer do so. Perhaps all of us should take another look at the men and women on the ground and in the air who chose to give their lives so that others might live.

Here, we can include the passengers on board United Airlines Flight 93, who staged a mutiny that ended in their death in Pennsylvania on that terrible day, but undoubtedly saved the lives of countless others. We can also include the courageous people on board the hijacked planes, who used their cell phones to share what was going on with courageous relatives and others who advised, comforted, and prayed with them.

Writing about the heroism of the crew and passengers of that ill-fated United Airlines flight brings to mind a more recent heroic airline incident with a happier ending. I'm thinking of the courage displayed by those involved in what is now known as the miracle on the Hudson. Shortly after takeoff from LaGuardia Airport during midafternoon on January 15, 2009, United Airways Flight 1549 experienced a rare "double bird strike." The Airbus A320 jetliner was under the command of Captain Chesley B. Sullenberger III.

Within minutes after takeoff, Captain Sullenberger—who is also a glider pilot—made the decision to make an emergency river landing with his disabled and powerless jetliner. This remarkable man now has also landed in the aviation history books for his amazing calm and cool courage, extraordinary competence, self-discipline, and many other winning traits.

But it was not only the masterful and safe river landing by this heroic pilot that made news headlines, but it was also the courage and wherewithal of crew members and passengers and the rescue workers who were quickly on the scene. Noteworthy among noteworthy events is that the pilot disembarked only after twice checking the jetliner, making sure not one of the 155 passengers and crew members was left behind. The events of that day were yet another reminder that human beings, endowed by their Creator with faculties of realism, reason, faith, and other abilities, are indeed God's marvel of marvels!

Perhaps we should remind ourselves, once again, that in whatever form courage comes, it presents itself as a virtuous choice. A choice of good over evil, courage over cowardice, winning over losing, and overcoming challenges rather than being overcome by them!

Remember These Points:

- Courage is at the heart of every virtue. In the absence of courage, it is highly unlikely to find an authentic winner.
- Authentic winners, as defined in this book, not only embrace a winning attitude and winning personality, but also wholesome—virtuous—goals.
- History is filled with examples of courageous winners who helped eradicate devastating illnesses, saved the lives of millions of people, furthered the ideals of democracy, equality,

freedom, and liberty; and in many other ways brought light and hope to those in darkness and despair.

- Authentic winners—regardless of age, gender, or race—have shown throughout history that there is no winning in life without the greatest of all virtues: courage.
- The courage of even one person—for example, Reginald Mitchell of Spitfire fame—can truly alter the course of history and directly affect multiple millions of people.
- It may take great courage to love those whose love for us, in one way or another, may have fallen short.
- The courage of those with physical and emotional health challenges and limitations is often legendary. It reminds us that it's not what we lack that defines us, but who we are and what we achieve with what we have.

13

Winners Are Disciplined

It is difficult to imagine a true winner who is undisciplined. To succeed in an age of information overload and endless distractions, it is crucial to have a disciplined mind. It requires a good amount of self-control to do only one thing at a time when there are so many things that seemingly must be done. Even very intelligent people may fail in their chosen careers if they lack the ability to concentrate on one project—or even one aspect of it—at a given time.

Self-Discipline Requires Concentration

Once we have made a realistic and rational decision to do something, it is necessary to focus on bringing it to pass. It is not so much lack of intelligence or interest, but focused effort that prevents many individuals from succeeding. All too often people fail because they are involved in far too many things at once. If you have a good occupation or profession, put all your effort into it and refuse to be sidetracked by those who want to draw you into their camp.

It is far better to be fluent in one language than to have only a scattered knowledge of many and fluency in none.

And obviously, it is better to be successful in one business than mediocre in two or three. A recent article, "The Secret to Raising Smart Kids," in *Scientific American Mind*, by Carol S. Dweck (2008), has pointed out that several decades of research has clearly revealed that it is focused effort, rather than one's ability or intelligence, that leads to success whether in school or in life. Interestingly, Cicero (106 BC-43 BC), the great Roman orator, already two thousand years ago, said that paying careful attention to one thing may well prove superior to genius. And we should not overlook that Ralph Waldo Emerson (1803-1882) pointed out that human power increases by wholehearted perseverance.

Self-Discipline Is Necessary for Personal Freedom

Self-discipline is not something we are born with. We slowly acquire it over time, once we realize that we can't be happy, healthy, or successful without it. Discipline involves goal setting and time management. All too often people are controlled by time—rather than being in control of it. Unless we budget time for professional, personal, and other uses—much like a financial budget—we may become slaves to unrealistic and often worthless projects. Worse, we may find that our mental, emotional, social, marital, and physical health is impeded by those misdirected actions.

It is important that we know what to do not only with the day at hand but also with our lives. Rational people don't waste time buying things piecemeal, making unnecessary trips, or allowing others to interrupt them during work hours with chitchat or meaningless events. Disciplined individuals don't wait until the very last minute to do something, go somewhere, or put something away. Our own work interruptions, of course, can be as bad as those we endure from others.

Many people believe their lives are being controlled by demands others place on them: interruptions they don't want, mail they didn't ask for, and so forth. But the truth is that we mostly control ourselves. "No one is free," cried Epictetus (60 AD-138 AD), "who is not master of himself." *Self-discipline is the key to personal freedom and personal power. Those who fail to conquer themselves are sitting ducks for failure and defeat, while those who conquer themselves are poised for success and victory.*

Self-Discipline Is a Choice

Victory in life doesn't exist apart from self-discipline and self-denial. A perceived absence of ability or strength is all too often only a lack of will. Many persons with addictive habits may have no desire to give them up, yet claim that they are unable to do so. Wilhelm von Humboldt got it right when he said that in the moral world there is nothing impossible if we *will* to do it. When the price is right—e.g., to save one's life—nearly all who previously were "unable" to give up some addiction, or other self-defeating habit, are now able to do so. I have frequently seen how seemingly intractable emotional problems could be overcome once an individual found it to be "worthwhile."

Victory comes more readily to us if we are willing to deny ourselves some comfort or pleasure and stay focused on the task at hand. Countless warriors—from Hannibal, Napoleon, Washington, Grant, Pershing, and Eisenhower to MacArthur—could attest to self-discipline as a requirement for success. In the pursuit of their goals, winners often must endure shivering cold or blistering heat.

Whether in peace or war, winning requires discipline. With the right moral fortitude, it is possible to overcome some of the most difficult challenges in one's life. Ultimately, discipline is a matter of character and temperament. The world of a true winner is a world of realism, reason, and optimism; a world not built by slackers but by disciplined and motivated doers.

Remember These Points:

- It is difficult to find an authentic winner who is not disciplined.
- Many people fail to succeed in their educational or vocational pursuits because they are involved in too many other unrelated events at once.
- It is far better to be skilled in one activity than mediocre in many.
- Self-discipline requires goal setting, focused effort, and time management.

- In the moral world, nothing is impossible if we will to do it.
- It is usually lack of focused effort, rather than lack of intelligence or interest, that prevents young and old alike from succeeding in school or life.
- More than two thousand years ago, Cicero, the great Roman orator, stressed that paying attention to just one thing may prove superior to genius.
- It is a common irrational belief that we are being controlled by the demands of others rather than by ourselves.
- Self-discipline is the key to personal freedom and personal power. Only those who conquer themselves can succeed in life.
- A victorious life does not exist apart from self-denial and self-discipline. Success is possible if a person wills to achieve it and stays focused on the task at hand.
- With the right moral fortitude, it is possible to overcome some of the most difficult challenges in our life.

14

Winners Are Doers

Winners are keenly aware that after *discerning, desiring,* and *deciding* must come the *doing*. Once they have decided to do something, they look for the first available opportunity to start because they refuse to do tomorrow what they can do today.

Meet a Need and You Succeed

Every successful person, in whatever endeavor, is a participator rather than a spectator. They are on the alert for opportunities and quick to seize them. Interestingly, most opportunities can be found right where we live and work. Carlyle said that we must not look at what lies dimly at a distance, but what lies clearly at hand. It is well-known that many individuals make their fortunes close to home by meeting the everyday needs of their community. Needs for shelter, food, and clothing, but also for education, health, and recreation.

If you are interested in starting a business that is most likely to succeed, you must consider not only your abilities, motivation, and other resources, but also your own needs. You may find that the needs of other people are similar to yours. Meet their needs and you'll succeed. Many successful entrepreneurs started very small, often working at first out of basements, homes, garages, or even garden sheds. Most successful individuals in our society worked hard with their own heads and hands; focused effort is the primary key to success!

Authentic Winners Are Self-Made Persons

"'Tis a common proof," said William Shakespeare, "that lowliness is young ambitious ladder." And so it is indeed. Most successful individuals started with hardly any financial resources. It is a myth that most successful people are born with a silver spoon in their mouth. In most cases, winners are self-made. The whining we sometimes hear from those who are less successful than others usually has no substance to it.

Procrastination Is an Enemy of Success

There are a number of negative habits that prevent many individuals from succeeding in life. High on this list we find procrastination and other aspects of poor time management. Procrastination may not only rob us from being a successful person, it may also rob us from enjoying our life. While we are postponing, life goes on. Common reasons for procrastination are found in negative self-talk and lack of self-esteem. As a result, procrastinators often prefer easy tasks over challenging ones, enjoyable ones over unpleasant ones, and to put things off until the last moment.

To overcome procrastination, it is necessary to be scrupulously honest with ourselves and take a close look at our personality style. There is a good possibility that we may have an *avoidant, compulsive, dependent, or negativistic personality style,* which may include fear of failure, perfectionism, overdependence, or passive-aggressiveness. In addition to overcoming self-defeating personality traits, as explained in chapter 24, we could embrace the following rules:

Anti-Procrastination Rules

- Time is the most precious resource I have. I refuse to squander it with aimless activities, unnecessary interruptions, collecting worthless objects, complaining about yesterday, or worrying about tomorrow. I guard against spending too much unproductive time on the phone or Internet.

- I work on one project at a time. My desk or work area is kept free from unrelated work. I work and live in an organized and uncluttered environment. I do things in order of importance and not level of difficulty. My daily goals are spelled out on paper and kept in view.

- I understand that the three most important rules for overcoming procrastination are the following: (1) do it now, (2) do it now, and (3) do it now.

It has been said that procrastination is a thief of time, possibilities, and opportunities. The same can be said of habitual idleness or wanton laziness. Those who wait until the last minute to complete a task or catch the last plane or train may find themselves last in many other things as well. The early bird truly does get the worm and late arrivers may go hungry. Punctuality and promptness are some of the many positive traits that set winners apart from others.

Sir Walter Raleigh, Sir Walter Scott, Frederick the Great, G. W. Leibnitz, and Napoleon Bonaparte are just a few of a myriad of well-known superachievers who were anything but procrastinators. Leibnitz (1646-1716), the famous German mathematician and philosopher, believed that losing an hour is like losing part of life. This doesn't mean that we cannot or should not have time for fun, recreation, relaxation, and so forth. These things are, of course, very important and will enhance and perhaps lengthen our lives.

Strong Reasons Make Strong Actions

There is no question whatsoever that all winners are doers, but it does not mean they rush into things. It's not haste and hurry that sets them apart, but promptness and punctuality. How can we move from dillydallying to making the most of our time? We could start by taking a good look at our self-talk. If we are given to pessimistic self-talk, we need to replace this with optimistic self-talk.

What motivates us more than anything else is the manner in which we perceive and interpret the world around us. We do things because we believe they are worth doing. If you know what you want to get away from, and know where you want to go, then it's time to stop the foot-dragging and start making some history. Procrastination is sometimes a sign of an emotional conflict, such as a fear of success—or more likely fear of failure, humiliation, or shame. While it is wise to seek professional help for this, it is sometimes important to just go through the fire. This can be done by starting with a small project (*one* phone call, *one* college class, *one* tiny speech) before moving on to more challenging events.

Goal Setting Is Important

Goal setting is very important for lasting success; many people don't plan to fail but fail to plan. The more clearly we define our goals, the more we are assured of reaching them. It is good to write down some of the important goals in your life. As you make a list of your long-term goals, be sure to start with, "I want to stay alive as long and happily as possible." And when writing down some of your immediate and intermediate goals, think about *doing* things such as attending, completing, contacting, giving, reading, returning, reviewing, studying, visiting, watching, and so forth.

Please remember that many people fail to live life *today*, while they live in the hope of living their life *someday*. Seneca wisely observed that while we are postponing things, life speeds by. Unless we set goals, it speeds by into nowhere. *Life is now.* Each day is the very time that we need to enjoy life to the fullest—at work, home, and play. We must do so regardless of the environment or circumstances in which we find ourselves. The objective is to set realistic goals, plan our time wisely, and enjoy life. Time on earth is finite, only fools can afford to waste it.

Remember These Points:

- Successful individuals are nearly always consistent doers.
- Winners are participators rather than spectators.
- Opportunities for success in the world of work may be close at hand if we can meet the everyday needs of the community in which we live.
- The more clearly we define our goals, the more we are assured of achieving them.
- Winners are invariably self-made persons who early in life discovered the importance of focused effort and hard work.
- Procrastination is a major obstacle to success; negative self-talk and lack of self-esteem are possible sources.
- Motivation is an acquired disposition; people more readily do the things that they value or believe are worth doing.
- Life is always in the present. Each day we need to enjoy life to the fullest—at home, school, work, or play.

15

Winners Are Enthusiastic

It would be difficult to imagine someone like Henry Ford, Bill Gates, or any other winner, without enthusiasm. I have never met a winner who didn't have a good deal of vigor and zest for one thing or another, especially life itself. Enthusiasm has variously been described as an ardent zeal, ecstasy of mind, or exalted state. In whatever way we look at enthusiasm, we cannot escape the fact that it is a powerful feeling and motivator. Enthusiasm compels and inspires us to do many things we might otherwise not even think possible.

Enthusiasm Is Exuberance in Action

Enthusiasm directly influences our chances for success in life. It helps us to gain competence, confidence, and other character traits that are needed to tenaciously persevere when faced with challenges or adversities. Our enthusiasm is also an inspiration to others who are more likely to support us if we are enthusiastic rather than indifferent. Enthusiasm, to a great extent, is a matter of the heart, but it must be supported by a rational mind. Enthusiasm, like other winning traits, can be acquired by most human beings. It is not a prerogative of the few but a choice of the many. No one succeeds in this world without enthusiasm; happily, no thinking person is denied the opportunity to acquire it. One of the hallmarks of winners is that they always get up one more time. They remain enthusiastic about their dreams, goals, and visions. They also know, however, that it is normal to experience challenges and occasional setbacks. Those who make history will fail at times and may lose some battles, but in the end, they win the war.

Enthusiasm turns challenges into opportunities. Those who remain hopeful when faced with challenges or setbacks are more likely to succeed. "Defeat," writes Helen Keller, "is nothing to be ashamed of; it is routine in digging the gold of one's personality. I have known people of faith who were defeated times without number and with whom I never associated failure" (Keller 1940). Authentic winners embrace realism, cultivate reason, enjoy the fruits of their labor, and in other ways may find themselves enriched by the things of the material world. But they find their strength increased and spirits lifted by an enthusiasm that makes light of arduous tasks, turns obstacles into challenges, and translates problems into opportunities.

Enthusiasm is important for all human endeavors, and perhaps more so for those who are in sales or similar occupations. Enthusiastic sales persons who value the products or services they are selling usually find that these products and services sell themselves. All that is required of the salesperson is competence, honesty, and enthusiasm. Whether in our private life or the world of work, there is no substitute for common sense, and it makes good sense to be enthusiastic about the things we believe in and want others to believe in as well. Enthusiastic individuals are always more successful than their indifferent counterparts. It is enthusiasm that undergirds a person's motivation to remain steadfast, stick to fundamentals, and succeed where many others fail.

Artists, such as Titian and Michelangelo, often worked for many years on just one painting. Many authors have labored for several decades on their manuscripts. Robert Burton, the well-known Oxford scholar, enthusiastically worked for thirty years on his *Anatomy of Melancholy*. First published in 1621, this book is still in print today, nearly four hundred years later! Throughout human history, we find that authentic winners succeed because they are enthusiastic about the things they do in their occupational, personal, and social life.

Remember These Points:

- Enthusiasm compels and inspires us to do many things we might otherwise not think possible.
- Enthusiasm is an incredibly important acquired trait found in every authentic winner.
- Enthusiasm is not a prerogative of the few but a choice for most people.
- Enthusiasm has a powerful multiplier effect. It increases one's self-confidence and at the same time inspires others to have confidence in the enthusiastic person, who, in turn, becomes even more enthusiastic and confident.
- Enthusiasm undergirds our motivation to remain unwavering in the pursuit of our short-term and long-term goals.

16

Winners Are Grateful

Winners are grateful for their health—even if far from perfect. They are grateful for the material things they have—even if few in number. Winners are very different from whiners, who—even with good health, excellent income, and many other blessings—may complain about minute inconveniences, while they care less about the *billions* of individuals on this earth who are suffering because they don't have the barest of necessities. Whiners don't have time for the poor, sick, and hungry and are unlikely to support them or those who seek to help them.

Ungrateful people are too entangled with their own petty problems to be concerned with the 33,000 children who die each day from mainly preventable illnesses, or the 40,000 people in the world who are dying from hunger each day. Whiners can escape the pit of self-pity if they start looking beyond themselves; for example, by supporting such organizations as *Care, Doctors Without Borders, World Vision,* and similar benevolent organizations.

There Is No Wealth But Life

Individuals who are truly grateful for whatever they have—be it little or much—are more willing to reach out to others, often risking their own lives. Here, we are face-to-face with the highest form of love—a willingness to lay down one's own life so that others may live. We cannot be winners in life if we are not grateful for the very experience of life itself. One that is not found in what was or is to be, but in being selflessly connected to others in the present. We already have all we need, if only we share what we have. Winners appreciate the beauty of life and readily agree with John Ruskin, the great nineteenth-century art critic, who said, "There is no wealth but life." Your life and all of life is precious.

Winners are grateful for most things in their life. We find this well demonstrated in the life and work of the literary genius, Gilbert Keith (G. K.) Chesterton, who lived from 1874-1936. Chesterton said that he gave "grace" not merely before meals, but before concerts, dancing, painting, playing, plays, operas, reading, swimming, walking, and before he started to write. If only we would be more like this godly man, filled with gratefulness for all we have.

I believe it is also wise to heed the viewpoint of Epictetus, the famous Stoic philosopher, who maintained that sensible people do not grieve over what they don't have but rejoice over what they do have. And that is precisely what real winners actually do. Winners are always an active part of the solution rather than a passive part of the problem. Also, they are not just grateful *to* God and country for their blessings. They do something with their blessings *for* God and country and refuse to be in the grip of self-pity, self-blame, or other blame.

Remember These Points:

- Winners are grateful for whatever they have and readily reach out to others in need.
- Winners have a deep appreciation for life in all its forms.
- Winners are grateful for the very experience of life itself.
- Winners don't pine over what they don't have, but rejoice over what they do have.
- Winners are not just grateful to God and others, they actively do something for God and others.
- Authentic winners are the heart and soul of any prosperous society that is concerned with the well-being of all.

17

Winners Are Honest

It has been said that it's not really possible to succeed in life if a person is honest. However, this is just another myth. Abraham Lincoln—an all-time winner—was known as Honest Abe for his legendary honesty. Authentic winners are scrupulously honest and have no need or desire to deceive anyone. They say what they mean and mean what they say. They make good on agreements, contracts, and promises; don't take advantage of others; have high ethical and moral standards; and follow reliable business practices.

Winners are not only honest with others but also with themselves. Although eager to succeed, for example, they will not set unrealistic goals. They pay close attention to what works and what does not work. If there's objective evidence that their thoughts, feelings, or actions are self-defeating, they seek to replace them with more life-enhancing ones. Authentic winners are alert also to the perils of mistaken persistence. They are too honest and rational to believe that it is always right to persevere to the end and perhaps find themselves bankrupt or worse. If they believe they are on the right track, however, winners will wholeheartedly persevere and get up one more time, every time.

Abraham Lincoln is a great example of a person who refused to be defeated. It was only through sheer diligence, tenacity, and perseverance that he became president of the United States and a leader of renown. Born in a tiny log cabin, without a floor or windows, on a stony hillside at Nolin's Creek, Kentucky—the son of a poor and illiterate father and a loving mother (and later a loving stepmother)—Lincoln was truly a self-made man. His word was as good as gold, and his social conscience was widely acclaimed.

Mental Mechanisms That May Hinder Honesty

Honesty is a highly desired trait, but it is important to know that there are mental mechanisms that seek to circumvent objective reality and honesty. These mechanisms include:

denial—An inability and sometimes a refusal to see the truth

displacement—The unconscious act of transferring negative emotive feelings from an unacceptable to an acceptable person or object

distortion—A misinterpretation of objective reality

idealization—An overestimation of someone else's admirable attributes

introjection—The unconscious act of symbolically absorbing within oneself (internalizing), feared, hated, or loved aspects of someone else.

projection—Unconsciously attributing our undesirable characteristics unto someone else.

rationalization—Explanation or justification of unacceptable, unrecognized, or irrational thoughts and actions.

reaction-formation—The unconscious management of one's unacceptable impulses by expressing them in an opposite form *repression*—The unconscious act of banishing unacceptable cognitions and emotive feelings from awareness

splitting—An evaluation of individuals in extremes; for example, someone is seen as all good or all bad, wonderful, or terrible.

suppression—The conscious act of banishing unacceptable cognitions and emotive feelings from awareness

Remember These Points:

- Authentic winners are scrupulously honest with others as well as with themselves.
- Authentic winners are alert to the perils of persistence; they only persevere if they know to be on the right course.
- The word "honesty" comes from the Latin *honestas*, meaning honor. More than a winning trait, honesty is essential for personal excellence, occupational success, and any healthy relationship or successful undertaking.

18

Winners Are Motivated

I have never seen anyone change his or her life for the better, or achieve something worthwhile, without a good dose of motivation. Motivation is the catalyst or stimulus that moves us into action and enables us to get something or get away from something. Without strong desire, there is no thoughtful action or winning in life.

Healthy and Unhealthy Motivation

Not all motivation is the same. It can, for example, be of the healthy or unhealthy variety. Many pseudowinners are stuck on the unhealthy kind, one that focuses on such idols as power and privilege. Such an outlook, however, all too often reaps the debility and disadvantage of a meaningless and joyless existence.

Healthy motivation, on the other hand, focuses on such wholesome goals as peace, freedom, democracy, justice, serenity, and tranquility. It furthers societal excellence with the development of such traits as altruism, courage, enthusiasm, honesty, and self-discipline. Healthy motivation builds healthy personalities, strengthens relationships, and gives dignity to our daily life and work.

Unhealthy motivation is the kind of motivation that is sometimes induced by "inspirationalists" who seek to bamboozle us into believing that we are the greatest, and that we and every other "greatest" sitting next to us can become millionaires and billionaires in the very near future. And while we are dancing for joy in our newly discovered *superior persona*, the inspirationalists are laughing all the way to the bank. The sad truth is that all too many individuals pay exorbitant prices for so-called secret of success lectures that are often no more than expensive sideshows.

Unhealthy motivation may cause excessive stress in your life, undermine your health, destroy your relationships, and leave you empty-handed and empty-headed at the end of the day. Why? Perhaps it is because you may have come to believe that you not only can but must also have everything in life. While it is true that you can have a winning attitude, winning personality, and much success in life, you cannot have everything. And you shouldn't want *anything* that diminishes you as a person, distracts you from doing what is right, or discourages your loved ones. *Healthy motivation gives you more than a good living, it gives you a good life!*

Motivation—within the context of this book—is simply one of the desirable traits of a winning personality. However, we must never overlook that individuals are often motivated (impelled/induced) by various events that originate outside the realm of our cognitions (attitudes, beliefs, thoughts, etc.). Here I am thinking, for example, about biochemical and other events, including nutritional, neurological, or other health challenges, not to mention powerful psychosocial and spiritual events.

Yet—and again within the context of this book—none of this means there is never any modification, regulation, or even rejection, of these or other physical sources by the very powerful mental and spiritual aspects of the triune nature of human beings. In other words, when it comes to motivation, I believe that mind, if not more than matter, is certainly no less than matter, and that, ultimately, our spiritual nature—attuned to God's spirit—will prove triumphant when it comes to our physical nature.

Remember These Points:

- Positive motivation is the catalyst that connects a person's winning attitude with other action steps needed for lasting success in life.
- Our motivation can be for good or evil. We can make a clear distinction between *unhealthy* and *healthy* motivation. The

former may focus on control, power, and privilege, but the latter focuses on wholesome goals that include both personal and social excellence.

- Unhealthy motivation is self-centered and stressful. It may undermine health, destroy relationships, and ultimately, leave us empty-handed and empty-headed.
- Healthy motivation provides far more than a good living, it provides a good life.
- There are many sources and causes of positive human motivation but the most powerful source is divine inspiration (cf. epilogue).

19

Winners Are Role Models

Authentic winners are powerful role models who often influence the behavior, future, and lifestyle of other individuals. As for myself, I have been inspired by such role models as my parents and individuals such as Ben Carson, John Foppe, Helen Keller, Phillippe Pinel, Albert Schweitzer, Joni Eareckson Tada, Corrie ten Boom, Mother Teresa, Nelson Mandella, and many others. Not to mention those who have set the ultimate example—risking life and limb for my physical freedom—or the Lord Himself, who freely gave His life for my spiritual freedom. In this chapter, however, I want to focus on some historical figures from this country: America—a mighty bastion of great ideals such as equality, freedom, and liberty.

Societal Excellence Requires Good Role Models

It is no accident that the United States has become a very powerful nation, and it is not by osmosis that we have so many real winners in this country. One of the more fundamental reasons for America's greatness can be found in the work ethic and religious values of its people, past and present. A society's excellence is, of course, only a reflection of the personal excellence of its members. In this country, from its earliest beginnings, we can find a great number of individuals who pursued wholesome goals and refused to quit even when the going was very tough at times.

Even a rudimentary glance at our socioeconomic, political, or cultural history—albeit, not without its faults and failures—reveals that we have been blessed with numerous individuals who are great role models of *competence, courage, determination, industriousness, motivation, leadership,* and *vision.* Leaders like George Washington, John Paul Jones, Benjamin Franklin, Patrick Henry, Abraham Lincoln, Ronald Reagan, Franklin D. Roosevelt, John F. Kennedy, Martin Luther King Jr., and scores of others. And let's not forget the many less-well-known or unknown winners who have contributed in equal and even greater measure to our day-to-day well-being—especially those who have sacrificed, or are sacrificing, life or limb for our daily freedom!

As we look at role models, it is necessary to recognize that media role models are not always good role models. Many of these individuals are cast into role model positions by marketers and other *hired hands.* Powerful self-interest groups spend billions of dollars to create illusionary role models so that millions of unwary individuals will buy products that carry the name or signature of some well-known person. There are, of course, some very good role models in the world of sports and entertainment but far too many are confusing especially our young people about values: distract them from their studies, nudge them into destructive behaviors, and empty their pocketbooks.

I think it is important to remember the *leadership* of George Washington, *bravery* of John Paul Jones, *determination* of the Wright brothers, *honesty* of Abraham Lincoln, *tenacity* of Helen Keller, *courage* of Rosa Parks, *philanthropy* of John D. Rockefeller, *industriousness* of Thomas Edison, and so many other good role models. If we are interested in succeeding in the twenty-first century, we are wise to take a close look at some of the outstanding role models of the eighteenth, nineteenth, and twentieth century. We'll soon find that they are still very relevant for this day and age.

I have mentioned the names of a few great Americans as a reminder that no great nation comes about by accident. And clearly, no nation can maintain its greatness by accident. "I never did anything," said Edison, "worth doing by accident, nor did any of my inventions come by accident." Surely, it was not by accident that Edison was not only a very generous person, but one of great competence, determination, discipline, enthusiasm, patience, and vision. Edison is an authentic winner who embraced a *winning attitude, winning personality*, and *wholesome goals*!

Authentic winners, however, are not only in demand as examples to follow, but also as the kind of individuals that people want to associate with. You may have noticed how they seem to just naturally and spontaneously gravitate toward positions of leadership. One reason is that they attract people toward them.

No wonder we have so many individuals and organizations who teach individuals how they can influence others. However, I have never been overly impressed with this approach. Not only because of ethical and social concerns, but also because in the long run, it simply doesn't work. Influencing techniques are not the most effective or most lasting way to have people get along with you or acquire your products or services on a long-term basis.

Motivation in the World of Work

One reason why so many companies have an endless series of pep rallies is because they try to maintain a certain level of motivation and enthusiasm in their staff. However important this may be for the success of a company, it falls far short of what could be achieved if these sessions were augmented with more in-depth training in the psychology of relationships. In the world of work, there is often a lack of knowledge on how *permanent* success can be attained. Do pep rallies work at all? Yes, but only for *temporary* success.

The reason why inspirational and motivational sessions continue to be held is quite obvious. Because of these sessions, many attendees change their negative perceptions, thoughts, and feelings into positive ones. They go back to work and increase their sales, but soon are back to square one. Once again, they lose heart and are in need of another tune-up. I call this event the "dipping-mood, dipping-sales" phenomenon.

Here is what happens. Someone attends a motivational session and alters his or her *thoughts* and even some *beliefs*, but what is not altered are underlying *attitudes*. These are not changed and cannot be changed in a training session. A new attitude is only slowly formed with much conscientious practice. It requires an understanding of what attitudes are and how they are changed (as explained in part 1 of this book). Only well-learned and habitually practiced beliefs will eventually become attitudes.

Another important aspect of the "dipping-mood, dipping-sales" phenomenon is that it may not only affect sales staff but also their customers. The latter are—as a rule—more ready to obtain goods and services from an enthusiastic and positive person than an indifferent and negative one. Most individuals are directly affected by the attitudes and moods of those with whom they come into close contact—and that includes both business and professional relationships.

Many companies make up for the loss of customers with more rallies and incentives. Again, we find a rise in the mood of the sales force, often even to hypomanic levels. The sales persons go out, find new customers, and for a while, sales will go up again. Of course, it is well-known that without advertising and "shaking the bushes," not much takes place in the selling of anything, regardless of how good a product or service may be. What continues to be overlooked, however, is that if we truly meet the needs of others—for example, by sincerely caring for people—they will more likely be associated with us on a near permanent basis!

Love Literacy and the World of Work

The key to successful relationships—including in the world of business and commerce—is found in our personality style. To be a successful role model and have others attracted to you requires there is *real substance* in you to be attracted to in the first place. In authentic winners, we find this not only in their winning attitudes and personalities, but also in high standards of decorum and wholesome goals, such as a well-developed social conscience and selfless love. These qualities make authentic winners ideal role models and the kind of people we want to associate with, whether at home, school, or the world of work.

But there is even more to this story. For example, authentic winners understand that their own sense of personal worth (based on love, achievement, and autonomy) can only be met and maintained by helping others to also have a true sense of personal worth.

Authentic winners know that helping others merely as a quid pro quo gesture is not only wrong, but a waste of time. True role models have true staying power. Consider the authentic winners I have mentioned in this chapter. Some of them lived a long time ago, yet their influence continues to be felt today. The life and work of Helen Keller, for example, inspires countless individuals around the globe to this very day and will always continue to do so.

Remember These Points:

- Authentic winners not only have been inspired by excellent role models but are also likely to become role models themselves.
- America has been blessed by many great role models with winning traits such as competence, courage, determination, leadership, and vision.
- In the world of work it is important to grasp that permanent success is more readily achieved by those who sincerely care for others and help meet their needs.
- A society's excellence is only a reflection of the excellence of its members.
- Religious values and a solid work ethic have directly contributed to America's greatness as a nation.
- Love literacy is the ultimate staying power of every authentic winner and every successful nation.

20

Winners Are Successful

"Success," I wrote elsewhere, "is not an end product, but a journey. A journey of dreams, goals, and visions. To be successful means living our dreams, going after our goals, using our talents, joyfully facing challenges, and tenaciously overcoming obstacles" (Brandt 1988). I believe that these insights correspond with those of John Maxwell, a well-known writer and expert on leadership, who also points out that true success is not necessarily something we "finally" acquire or achieve, but that it is a journey for life. Maxwell wisely suggests that we give time and energy only to the themes that lie at the heart of our life, know our purpose in life, work toward our maximum potential, and sow seeds that benefit others (Maxwell 2002).

Authentic Success Is Based on Wholesome Values

True success is far more an intrinsic than an extrinsic matter. It is a matter of the heart in pursuit of ethical, moral and/or religious values such as altruism, goodness, honesty, integrity, justice, and so forth. Winners want to achieve constructive and meaningful goals: peace of mind, contentment, satisfying relationships, and a happy home life. They want to succeed in their chosen careers and occupations, but only as part of a larger picture. One that embraces a purposeful and meaningful life.

All this is quite different from what we find in those whose road map to success is narcissistically and narrowly focused only on themselves and the accumulation of power, prestige, and privilege.

These individuals may give little thought to societal excellence or wholesome goals. Many of them appear to be first in the race, including some CEOs of major corporations, financial institutions, and so forth. Sadly, all too many of them are only in a rat race. They all too willingly bend the rules and never have enough!

Short on meaning and purpose in life, increasingly obsessed by never having enough material wealth, and in a perpetual frenzy to get more and more done in less and less time, they fall victim to what Dr. Paul Pearsal (2002) calls "toxic success." He found that these individuals become disconnected from themselves and lose all capacity for emotional intimacy. Not a great picture of success!

Authentic success—wholesome success—is not possible without sensibly caring for our physical, emotional, social, and spiritual health. If we live in a chronic state of *discontentment, aimlessness,* and *excessive stress,* we are, obviously, not successful. Success is not only a journey, but it's also an adventure to enjoy in the here and now, rather than only at some future date. Success is more than savoring a moment of glory found at the end of a harsh pilgrimage through life.

I believe a successful (flourishing) life is a meaningful, purposeful, and tranquil life. Its *meaningfulness* is defined by a deeply felt sense of personal worth—related to some measure of achievement and autonomy—and enduring, loving relationships; its *purposefulness* by realistic and rational ambitions, hopes, and goals; and its *tranquility* by habitual calmness, contentment, harmony, patience, and gentleness.

Remember These Points:

- Authentic success is not an end product but a journey in pursuit of realistic dreams and wholesome goals—a journey to be fully enjoyed in the here and now.
- Authentic success requires solid traits such as competence, determination, enthusiasm, and focused effort, as well as a benevolent philosophy of life.

- Authentic success also requires that we sensibly care for our physical, mental, emotional, and spiritual health. There are no dividers between body, mind, and spirit.
- A successful life is an integrated and well-balanced life: solidly *purposeful,* deeply *meaningful,* and habitually *tranquil.*

21

Winners Are Tenacious

Not every winner has the same number of winning traits or has them to the same breadth and length as some other winner. Yet if there is one trait that is typical of virtually every winner, it is the will to stick things out and cling to dreams, goals, and visions. Tenacious perseverance is what makes winners hang tough when storm clouds gather, when many others are in full retreat or austerity is on the order of the day.

Tenacity Thrives on Trouble

Authentic winners know that perseverance in the pursuit of a wholesome goal will pay off. One such winner, *Winston Churchill* (1874-1965), as prime minister of Great Britain during World War II, told his followers to "never ever give up." His legendary tenacity was instrumental in maintaining the freedom of his country and eventually help the Allied powers secure victory over Nazi Germany.

One of Churchill's most famous speeches (we shall fight on the beaches) was given in the House of Commons, June 4, 1940. Harold Nicolson, a member of Parliament at that time, had this to say about the speech and the man who gave it: "I think that one of the reasons why one is stirred by his Elizabethan phrases is that one feels the whole massive backing of power and resolve behind them, like a great fortress they are never words for words' sake" (Nicolson 1967). And that's precisely the way it is. There is no stopping a winner whose mind and body is wholeheartedly in pursuit of a wholesome goal.

As I am writing these remarks about one of Britain's great prime ministers, Winston Churchill, my mind is wandering off to some other tenacious British prime ministers. Individuals such as *William Ewart Gladstone* (1809-1898), the openly devout British political leader whose competence and tenacity earned him four terms as prime minister and—more importantly—secured voting by secret ballot and elementary education for all the children of Great Britain; and *Margaret Thatcher* (1925-) who stuck to her beliefs in a central government, free market, and self-reliance. Her courageous stand against the former Soviet Union—among other events—earned her the nickname of Iron Lady.

In more recent history, we must not overlook British Prime Minister *Tony Blair* (1953-), who has tenaciously held his own against the forces of darkness—both at home and abroad. He was one of the first world leaders to stand shoulder to shoulder with the grieving people of the United States in its forced defense against terrorism. More recently, we find that the deeply religious former British prime minister has turned his attention—and the full weight of his tenacity—to the urgent need for more harmony and understanding between the major religions of the world (Elliott 2008). As we look at political leaders such as Gladstone, Churchill, Thatcher, and Blair, we can readily observe their incredible tenacity.

The American poet, Henry Wadsworth Longfellow (1807-1882), clearly believed in the power of perseverance when he wrote this:

> Let us, then, be up and doing,
> With a heart for any fate;
> Still achieving, still pursuing,
> Learn to labor and to wait.

Longfellow understood that every achievement of note takes hard work over extended periods. Just consider how long it takes to enter one of the professions, whether it's in the arts, sciences, or the world of sports. It takes many years of intensive labor to become a ballerina, opera singer, Olympic champion, national political leader, physician, or whatever else. To earn a doctoral degree may require as much as ten full years of college and several additional years of work to become proficient in a professional field.

A lot of hype to the contrary, there is no such thing as authentic success in life without focused effort and hard work. Only those who are tenacious enough to stick things out over the long haul succeed in life. The formation of any useful character trait takes time and effort. If we look closely at the lives of winners, we find they have one weakness or another, but lack of tenacity is never one of them.

Not Every Winner Is at the Same Level of Development

As we conclude our review of some of the more common winning personality traits, it is best not to overlook that every person is unique. No one, of course, has the same field of awareness, window of opportunity, or winning traits to the same degree. In some respects, all winners are quite similar to each other, but in other respects, they are very dissimilar, or at least somewhat dissimilar from one another. There are many genetic, biochemical, and environmental reasons why every winner—and every human being—is unique and at different levels of development.

While it seems clear that most authentic winners are similar because they have—broadly speaking—a winning attitude, winning personality style, and wholesome goals, it is perhaps even more clear that they are dissimilar in many respects. They have different ethnic, racial, social, cultural, economic, religious, and other backgrounds; they are male and female, young and old, and have different talents, hopes, dreams, and visions. Yet in one thing, all winners remain very much alike: in the pursuit of their wholesome goals, they are sure to get up one more time, every time.

Remember These Points:

- Authentic winners have an unwavering commitment to wholesome goals even in the midst of great hardships.
- Famous British winners—such as Churchill, Gladstone, Thatcher, and Blair—translated powerful words into powerful

actions, affirming that "death and life is in the power of the tongue."

- Longfellow, the beloved American poet, observed that achievements of note take concentrated effort over extended periods of time.
- Authentic winners tenaciously pursue their dreams, goals, and visions.
- The formation of winning character traits takes both effort and time.
- All winners are similar in their commitment to get up one more time, every time.

PART THREE

WINNERS HAVE WHOLESOME GOALS

22

Winners Have a Healthy Social Conscience

Individuals with a healthy social conscience are interested in the welfare of all people. They will do whatever they can to make the community and the world in which they live a better place. The presence of a social conscience is often seen in small things, such as common courtesies or other forms of civilized behavior. Those who have a social conscience show this in a great variety of contexts. It may be in the form of financial contributions, free professional services, sharing of belongings, volunteer work, and so forth.

Don't Discount Small Deeds

One place where you may readily see the presence—or absence—of a social conscience is at your local supermarket. Upon arrival at the parking lot, you may find that a number of shopping carts are located all over the place. Sometimes making it difficult for you to safely park your car without first moving some abandoned shopping carts. Most of these are left behind by people who were perfectly fit to bring their groceries to their cars but apparently not fit enough to place an empty cart in a cart corral or return the cart to the store. What is the big deal here? The big deal is that it shows a disregard for others and especially for mothers with children and older or infirm individuals. Not to mention a disregard for the store clerks who have to keep rounding up discarded carts all day long in all kinds of weather.

Once inside the supermarket, you may find further evidence that some of the shoppers have a rather careless attitude toward their fellow shoppers. They may block an aisle and ignore your pleading eyes or repeated attempts to circumnavigate the blockage. Rather than confront someone who perhaps lacks a social conscience, you'll probably go to the next aisle in the hope that the problem will have resolved itself upon your return.

While you are at the supermarket, you may be able to see many other small manifestations of carelessness. For example, individuals who are deftly walking around objects that have fallen off some shelf. "Why in the world," they seem to say, "would I want to pick that stuff up?" And then there are those who change their mind about something they had earlier placed in their cart. Rather than returning the item to its proper location, they will simply stuff it anywhere. Why in the world would someone go to all the trouble of returning the frozen bologna to the frozen food section, while it fits perfectly fine between the light bulbs?

There are, of course, many far more serious examples that can be found to show the absence of a social conscience. But we really don't need to do this. It's a simple fact of life that most of those who fail socially in small matters are more likely to also fail in large ones. And what is more, if we are interested in developing a better social conscience, we may have to start with small things.

Even seemingly small gestures, such as being helpful or friendly to a depressed or isolated person, have literally prevented suicides. Not to mention that even very small donations to worthy causes *are* saving millions of people from starvation. Never ever underestimate the importance of a social conscience.

Success Is a Two-way Street

Real winners, of course, have a social conscience and will stand alone if need be. Just take a look at Columbus. Considered a fool by many, he often stood alone. And so did many an inventor, from Samuel Morse (1791-1872) and Graham Bell (1847-1922) to Thomas Edison (1847-1931). Yet all authentic winners remain aware that they are an integral part of social institutions, communities, and society at large; and they sincerely want to contribute to them.

Winners know that success is only found on a two-way street. Ultimately, it's neither dependence nor independence that saves the day, but interdependence. "Give," we are told, "and you will receive." This also works in reverse. Those who receive must not forget to share with others and give something back to society. Concern for the welfare of others is more urgent today than ever before.

There are more than one billion individuals on earth who must exist on less than one dollar a day. Another two billion individuals must live on less than two dollars a day. This means that about 50 percent of the world's population lives on less than two dollars a day! We live in a world where twelve million young children die each year from mainly preventable causes. Please note that this translates into thirty-three thousand children under age five who needlessly die every day. Also, daily, tens of thousands of people die from hunger. We live in a world where one nation (Sierra Leone) has an average life expectancy of less than thirty years, while others—like Japan—have an average life expectancy of over eighty years. We live in a world where we use natural resources at a rate faster than the earth can replenish; a world that is clearly in need of caring people with a social conscience.

We also live in a world that is beset with crime, corruption, cultism, fanaticism, fatalism, ignorance, illiteracy, legalism, and terrorism. And in the middle of this wilderness, we find those who shamelessly prosper from suffering and vileness. These individuals are usually not too difficult to identify. But there are others—more difficult to distinguish—who may wrongfully present themselves as winners.

Please remember that authentic winners have a social conscience, in things large or small. I am happy and proud to live in a country where the good clearly outweighs the bad and where caring people greatly outnumber those who don't care. In our most recent history, there has been ample opportunity to witness the awesome and inspiring behavior of so many individuals who are truly among the greatest winners the world has ever seen. No one has a greater social conscience than those who risk life and limb to safeguard and rescue other people, or who fight for democracy, equality, and freedom. As we take a closer look at our own social conscience, we best remember those who continue to set the example and are willing to pay the ultimate price.

Remember These Points:

- A person with a social conscience cares for—and whenever possible supports—the well-being of other individuals.
- A person's social conscience, or lack thereof, is often quite apparent even in small things—such as deference, friendliness, helpfulness, lawfulness, and/or politeness.
- Concern for the welfare of others—here and abroad—is more urgent today than ever before.
- Those who fail socially in small things are quite likely to also fail in larger ones.
- Authentic winners usually have a strong social conscience.
- No one has a greater social conscience that those who will risk life and limb to safeguard and rescue other individuals.

23

Winners Have a Healthy Reverence for Life

One of the most inspiring facets of human history is found in the tireless and often heroic efforts of those who fight to enhance, protect, or save human life. Even a very rudimentary look at the lives of these individuals reveals that most of them are tried and true winners. In pursuit of such wholesome goals as banishing despair, ignorance, illness, and suffering, these inexhaustible champions of life always get up one more time.

Champions of Life

Champions of life are found in many human endeavors, but some of the best examples can be found in the history of medicine. Here we find the names of those who helped conquer deadly infectious diseases, lowered maternity and infant mortality rates, and developed surgical procedures that have saved life and limb of multiple millions of people.

I am thinking of Hippocrates (c. 460-c. 370 BC), the father of modern medicine, who freed medicine from the bondage of superstition and promoted a more scientific approach in the treatment of disease. I'm thinking of Galen (c. 130-c. 200 AD), the Greek court physician of the Roman emperor, Marcus Aurelius (121-180 BC). Galen wrote hundreds of treatises on his medical observations and findings—e.g., that arteries don't transport air but blood—and for over *one thousand years*, he remained the number one medical authority in the world. In more recent history, we find such notable physicians and scientists as Radcliffe, Mead, Askew,

Pitcairn, Curie, Pasteur, Salk, Fleming, Pinel, Pauling, Schweitzer, and scores of others. All had a tremendous reverence for life, but it was Albert Schweitzer who, perhaps, became its most outspoken proponent.

The Sacredness of Human Life

Advocates for the sacredness of human life, as I said earlier, can be found in many other fields, and this holds especially true for philosophy and theology. Throughout the ages, men and women have selflessly given their all to improve, protect and save human life, and reduce the suffering of others. Most noteworthy is that they don't just do this for a particular ethnic, racial, or religious group of people, but for *any* individual. Why? Undoubtedly, they do this for varied reasons, but one of the most powerful is the Judeo-Christian view that all human beings are created in the image of God and that life is precious.

Albert Schweitzer—a man of great faith and a loving soul—identified himself with *all* of humanity. A man who knew very well that serving others was far from easy. Yet he saw it as a privilege and the secret of true and lasting happiness. He also believed that it is only by example that we may hope to influence others. Already a renowned scholar, philosopher, theologian, and organist in the early twentieth century, he decided to turn his attention to the study of medicine and dedicate his life to helping sick and hurting people in Central Africa. His love for people and reverence for life soon became legendary and spread around the globe.

Dr. Schweitzer was born on January 14, 1875, at Kaysersberg, in the Upper Alsace of France, but he grew up in Gunsbach, which is located in the Münster Valley of Germany. At age nine, he was a stand-in church organist; at age eighteen, he studied theology *and* philosophy at the University of Strasbourg, France. At age twenty-four, he earned a doctorate in philosophy, and at age twenty-five, he became the vicar of St. Nicholai Church in Strasbourg. By age twenty-seven, he was teaching at his alma mater—the University of Strasbourg—and when only thirty years old, he was famous throughout Europe as an expert on organ building, organ playing, and the music of Johann Sebastian Bach. Here we find a highly respected young man with an incredibly bright future ahead of him, who decided to forgo a life of fame and fortune and enroll in medical school with no other objective than to become a jungle-doctor and help hurting people for the rest of his life—until he was ninety years old.

Albert Schweitzer is one of the most outstanding winners of all time. Author, humanitarian, musician, philosopher, physician, scientist, and theologian, Schweitzer worked day in and day out in his primitive Lambarene jungle hospital. But he also stayed in touch with the outside world seeking to help those who lived far beyond the borders of Central Africa. For his unrelenting efforts to create a more peaceful world, Dr. Schweitzer was awarded the Nobel Peace Prize in 1952. The stipend that came with this honor was promptly used to make improvements to his hospital and to build a leper colony.

Light Is Stronger than Darkness

Now let's contrast those who give their lives to save life with those who waste their lives to destroy life. Contrast those who have reverence for life with those who only have contempt for it. Look at terrorists, whether young or old, *American* (e.g., at Columbine, Oklahoma City, and workplaces throughout the country) or *foreign* (e.g., at the World Trade Center, Pennsylvania, and The Pentagon) who diabolically and ruthlessly maim or destroy anyone they don't like, stands in their way, or can be used for some pathological purpose. Blinded by the powers of darkness, they readily destroy the lives of others and themselves.

Violent people, religious zealots, and other disturbed individuals—filled with bitterness, envy, confusion, greed, hatred, or jealousy—have, since the dawn of history, been bamboozled by the powers of evil. Some even believe the diabolical lie that destroying innocent men, women, and children will be rewarded by a benevolent god—who teaches the exact opposite of what they are doing! Brainwashed, deceived, and hypnotized by the incantations and unscrupulous actions of diabolical leaders, these men and women have no hope, no future, no joy, no spring in their step, no song in their heart, and no mercy for anyone. The actions of terrorists are so self-defeating that they not only self-destruct as individuals but also their hoped-for goals suffer an equal or worse fate. Why? Because light is stronger than darkness. Evil cannot win over good. The work of those who have reverence for life will stand in glory, but the actions of those with contempt for life will vanish in shame.

Remember These Points:

- One of the most inspiring aspects of human behavior is seen in the tireless and heroic efforts of those who fight for the enhancement, protection, and safeguarding of human life.
- Champions of life abound in every area of human endeavor—especially in the field of medicine, philosophy, and theology.
- The Nobel Peace Prize winner, Dr. Albert Schweitzer—physician and all-time great defender of life—believed that the secret of true and lasting happiness is found in service to others.
- The actions of those who have contempt for the sacredness of life will vanish in shame, but the work of those who have a reverence for life will flourish.

24

Winners Have a Healthy Personality Style

One of the numerous benefits winners gain from fully embracing constructive thinking is the slow but sure development of not only a *winning* personality style but also of a *healthy* personality style. For authentic winners, the two simply go together! On the other hand, if someone's life is *dominated* by unrealistic, irrational, and/or negative thoughts and actions, that person is quite likely the owner of one or more of the following unhealthy personality styles:

Antisocial—Convincing, but often deceitful and uncaring.

Avoidant—Polite, but often hypersensitive and withdrawn.

Borderline—Gregarious, but often capricious and unsure.

Compulsive—Conscientious, but often critical and perfectionistic.

Dependent—Devoted, but often insecure and clingy.

Depressive—Serious, but often pessimistic and gloomy.

Histrionic—Romantic, but often dramatic and impulsive.

Narcissistic—Charming, but often egotistical and exploitive.

Negativistic—Autonomous, but often oppositional and vacillating.

Paranoid—Protective, but often hypervigilant and suspicious.

Self-defeating—Sacrificing, but often self-abasing and self-demeaning.

Schizoid—Modest, but often detached and unsociable.

Focus on Being a Constructive Person

In order to have a healthy personality style, you need to regularly practice constructive (realistic, rational, positive) thinking. In part 1 of this book and elsewhere (Brandt 1999, 2003), I've described how you can do this. Here are three things you must pay particular attention to:

- *Realistically validate your perceptions.* Separate fact from fiction and don't believe everything you hear. Set realistic goals and trade off short-term fleeting pleasures for solid long-term gains. Question your perceptions: "Is this accurate?" "Where is the evidence?" "How might others see this?" "What would a videotape recording show?" "How does this relate to other facts?"
- *Rationally evaluate your responses.* Do your responses help improve the quality of your life, achieve your goals, allow you to feel the way that you want to feel and keep you out of unwanted troubles? Remember that your thoughts literally determine how you feel and act: "Death and life are in the power of the tongue."
- *Optimistically focus on the very best in all circumstances of life.* Boldly move forward in hopeful expectation with your realistically discerned and rationally made decisions. Don't waver once the die has been cast; look back during liftoff or take your eyes off the goal that has been set.

Focus on Being an Adaptable Person

Foster *insightfulness* by accurately observing and carefully interpreting your motivations and actions. This often requires the courage to face unpleasant issues rather than to ignore or suppress them. Anatole France (1844-1924), the French literary giant and Nobel Prize winner, said, "We must die to one life before we can enter into another." It's this kind of enlightened insight that helps us to adapt to ever changing circumstances in life.

Foster *open-mindedness* by recognizing and admitting that you are a fallible and imperfect person who can be mistaken in the observation or interpretation of given facts or events. If appropriate, yield to another point of view or learn to do things in a new or better way.

Foster *flexibility* by knowing when to give or take, lead or follow, and accepting unpleasant facts or events without anger or bitterness. Always look at new challenges as opportunities rather than as hindrances.

Focus on Being a Caring Person

Foster *sharing* by considering the plight of those who are less prosperous or successful than you. Don't do this out of a sense of duty or need for recognition, but because you desire to be altruistic, compassionate, helpful, and generous as a matter of course.

Foster *forgiving* by quickly reaching out to those who make amends and seek pardon, and by not harboring anger, bitterness, or resentment toward those who are unable or unwilling to do these things. By so doing, you provide an opportunity for the healing of relationships, restoring peace, and bringing emotional release to yourself and others.

Foster *loving* others by fully accepting them—without bias or prejudice—regardless of ethnic, racial, social, religious, or other differences. Increasingly, appreciate, accept, respect, and put into practice that there are no inferior or superior people but only fallible and imperfect ones—starting, of course, with ourselves.

Individuals who embrace most of the traits I have just described are relaxed and peaceful individuals who are not easily offended or slighted. They have no need to manipulate, intimidate, or dominate anyone. They respect cultural, social, and other differences found in others and are able and willing to associate, cooperate, and work with them, without necessarily endorsing or supporting their philosophy of life.

Focus on Being a Comfortable Person

Foster *good feelings about yourself* and become increasingly relaxed about the inevitability of numerous uncontrollable, unexpected, and often unpleasant personal events that virtually affect everyone's life. Learn to chill out. Self-blame or self-pity only makes unpleasant events worse.

Foster *good feelings about others* and get along with them without insisting that they should or must get along with you. Never seek to control others; it is not only wrong, but sooner or later, it backfires—leaving you empty-handed. Instead, become an objective and patient listener, readily communicate your thoughts and feelings on a verbal and nonverbal level and respect cultural, ethnic, religious, and other differences.

Foster *good feelings about objective reality* by seeking to alter, reduce, or overcome unpleasant or harmful interpersonal and environmental conditions without dysfunctional anger, anxiety, or depression; change whatever can be changed and accept as calmly as possible that which cannot be changed.

Remember These Points:

- *Adaptable persons* deal with facts and events objectively and are aware of their own strengths and weaknesses.
- Adaptable persons consider the opinions of others, are open to suggestions for personal change, and look for new or better ways to do things.

- Adaptable persons can give or take, lead or follow, speak or listen, adjust to rapidly changing circumstances, and do not always have to be right.
- *Caring persons* gladly share their blessings with others, have a deep reverence for life and will support the common good.
- Caring persons harbor no anger, bitterness or resentment, but further the happiness and well-being of other people.
- Caring persons accept individuals of diverse backgrounds, recognize that all human beings are fallible and care for people in a selfless manner.
- *Constructive persons* seek to validate their perceptions.
- Constructive persons rationally evaluate their thoughts, create helpful feelings, and seek to live as long and happily as possible.
- Constructive persons confidently implement their reasonable choices and decisions, look for the best in every situation, and opt for calmness and confidence if humanly possible.
- *Comfortable persons* feel good (if ethically and rationally justified) about themselves and don't easily feel offended or rejected by others.
- Comfortable persons are able to associate and work with individuals of diverse backgrounds, without necessarily endorsing all or any of their beliefs and values.
- Comfortable persons view the world—in spite of its very often chaotic condition and appearance—as a place where nothing happens unless needed prerequisites have been met.
- Authentic winners—who have a winning as well as a healthy personality—are fully functioning, mature, interdependent, and solution-focused individuals. They are able to gratify their basic needs and find meaning and purpose in life by embracing a wholesome philosophy of life, such as selflessly serving God, family, and all of humanity.

25

Winners Have a Healthy Physical Lifestyle

Even with excellent health, it is not always easy to be a winner. But it is a great deal more difficult if we are in poor health. It really makes sense that so many winners are health conscious and fully committed to a healthy lifestyle. A lifestyle that is a help rather than a hindrance in the pursuit of their goals.

Most individuals would agree that winning in life requires a clear mind that can remember facts and events and make sound decisions. They would also agree that it is not possible to have a happy and healthy mind without a healthy brain. But they are less sure what it takes to have a healthy brain. For example, there seems to be a tendency to overlook that the brain needs sound nutrition!

Most Chemical Imbalances Are Lifestyle Related

It is frequently misunderstood, overlooked, or ignored that *most* mental and emotional difficulties are not just a matter of the mind or brain, but of the whole person. All too often, our bouts with anger, anxiety, confusion, depression, forgetfulness, restlessness, sleeplessness, sleepiness, and a host of other difficulties find their primary source in disturbed body/brain chemistry. For example, it is difficult, and sometimes impossible, to think right if our brain cells don't have certain nutrients because we failed to eat a healthy diet. *An unhealthy diet can literally prevent us from succeeding in life.*

Disturbed brain chemistry—a so-called biochemical imbalance in otherwise healthy or functional people—is rarely caused by organic brain disease. *Most of the time, the biochemical imbalance (for which no tests exist) is, in reality, a nutritional imbalance caused by a faulty diet and lifestyle.* Here, I'm thinking in particular of addictive, allergenic, and toxic substances, malnutrition and excessive stress (Brandt 2007).

One of the more common causes of the human brain going haywire results from insufficient blood glucose in the brain. A steady and sufficient supply of glucose, oxygen, and other nutrients is essential for proper brain functioning and a healthy mental and emotional life. *I believe that at least 25 percent of our population is directly at risk for glucose-related mental/emotional difficulties.* When low blood sugar problems in the brain are severe enough, there will be a host of signs and symptoms, including problems with concentrating, learning, and remembering. Without a steady and sufficient supply of blood sugar, the brain goes haywire. I've seen this over and over on an endless number of occasions and have mentioned this in several books (Brandt 1984, 1988, 1999, 2000, 2007).

Of course, it is important not to overlook that when our mind is sufficiently disturbed by self-defeating thoughts and beliefs that not only our brain but also our body chemistry will be disturbed. We are all too familiar with the many stress-related illnesses that plague millions of individuals. For example, elevated blood pressure, blood sugar and cortisol levels are often directly related to excessive stress.

Body and mind are interdependent, we don't have some convenient zipper to keep the mind, brain, and (rest of the) body safely apart. What affects one part will affect the other. I think that most people would agree that they are more likely going to succeed if they have a healthy body and mind. Nothing, it seems, distracts more from day-to-day happiness and success than the aches, pains, and other physical distractions of an ailing body. What can you do about this? A very great deal!

Most Illnesses Are Preventable

Unhealthy lifestyles are the real culprit behind most of the ailments with which people needlessly suffer. *Amazingly, 65 percent of all illnesses are due to diet alone, and 75-85 percent of all illnesses are actually preventable.* The leading killers in our society are cancer, cerebrovascular disease, chronic lung disease, and heart disease. Most cancer is directly related to the use of alcohol, diet, and tobacco, as well as certain environmental factors. Cerebrovascular disease is related to the use of tobacco, elevated blood pressure, excessive intake of dietary cholesterol, nutritional deficits, and/or a sedentary lifestyle. Chronic lung disease is related to the use of tobacco products and environmental pollution, including second-hand smoke. Heart disease has been linked primarily to tobacco, obesity, high cholesterol, inflammation and/or a sedentary lifestyle, and the list of preventable illnesses goes on and on.

Most Illnesses Are Curable

It is far easier to prevent illness than to cure it, but the good news is that most illnesses are curable, and that this can be achieved by mostly natural means. And just as the source for most illnesses is found in the use of a wrong diet—and other lifestyle issues—the cure for most illnesses is found in the use of the right diet and other lifestyle issues.

Please note that the emphasis in the previous paragraph is first on diet and only second on other lifestyle issues. This doesn't mean that you can neglect either one. You need a sound diet and a sound lifestyle to help prevent or cure illness. I mention diet first because it can often, by itself, do what no other lifestyle event can do by itself.

For example, many lifestyle events are harmful to vision—which may be impacted by disease, neurotoxins, trauma, and so forth. More likely, however, less dramatic events may gradually reduce your vision. These may include the following: free radicals from sunlight or other sources; reduced blood flow and lack of oxygen from smoking; lack of exercise; infectious agents and other environmental events. Yet in both the prevention and cure of these vision challenges, you cannot exclude the use of certain key nutrients found in a wellness-oriented diet that is at least mainly vegetarian and free of junk food and addictive substances (Brandt 2007).

Healing by natural means has since long been used for nearly all health challenges, including acidosis, allergies, anxiety, arthritis, arrhythmia, blocked arteries, cancer, constipation, depression, diabetes, heart disease, high cholesterol, inflammation, insomnia, memory loss, learning problems, obesity, migraines, and weight-control issues. When it comes to the prevention of disease, however, the list quickly gets a great deal longer.

Supernatural Healing Miracles

Do supernatural healing miracles exist? Before answering this question, I think it's important to share my conviction that a healthy physical lifestyle cannot be separated from a healthy emotional, or even a healthy spiritual lifestyle. I have discussed this in detail elsewhere (Brandt 1988, 2000, 2007). However, many individuals—including believers of various denominations—are often extremely reluctant to consider even the possibility of supernatural healing miracles.

In our modern world, lack of faith does not come as a surprise. Nowadays, many individuals find it difficult to believe even in the *natural* healing miracles that are taking place, en masse, with very simple nutritional and other natural approaches. Of course, it would be extra difficult for them to believe in *supernatural* healing miracles. This unbelief is probably to some degree an offspring of the germ theory, as espoused by the French chemist Louis Pasteur (1822-1895), and the overtly commercial influence of the Industrial Revolution. Both have fostered the belief that most illness is simply pathogen-driven and can (at least eventually) be cured by scientific medical interventions.

Having said all this, it's time to answer our earlier question. I hold that supernatural healings do indeed exist. For starters, I have personally received—and know others who have received—supernatural healings by faith. A direct gift, so to speak, from the hand of God. I hasten to add, however, that in my life and work experiences, the incidence of *supernatural* healing miracles is far less common than *natural* healing miracles. Why?

I think the message is clear: whenever possible, we are to help ourselves with the help God has already provided. For example, God's Word makes it rather clear how we are to live our lives and how we are to treat our bodies. From my admittedly limited theological vantage point, God is a God of health *and* healing. He has however placed before us the responsibility, as well as the means, to prevent and cure most health challenges by natural methods. I wholeheartedly believe that healing—whether by natural or supernatural means, medicine or surgery, or any combination of these—ultimately, is from the hand of God. With all this good news, it's time to consider some of the steps we can take toward a healthy physical lifestyle.

Some Important Steps toward a Healthy Lifestyle

I am firmly convinced that unhealthy lifestyles are also either the primary or secondary culprit behind most of our *mental/emotional problems*. To think and feel right, we must live right and vice versa. If our entire population set out to have a healthy lifestyle, we would soon find most hospital beds empty and most doctors looking for other employment. What is more, our accident, crime, and delinquency rates would drop dramatically. Rather than wait for this to happen on a national scale, it is best to start on a local scale: with ourselves. There is an ongoing controversy over what constitutes a healthy lifestyle, but most experts would fully agree that it includes weight control, exercise, sleep, a healthy diet, and abstention from addictive substances. Let's take a look.

- *Maintain Reasonable Weight*

One of the more insidious and destructive aspects of living in a fast-food society (one addicted to *fatty*, *salty*, and *sugary* foods) is the stealthily destruction of the happiness and health of millions upon millions of the most vulnerable people in this country. I am thinking about those who lack the education, training, and other resources necessary to effectively resist the hype, undue pressures, and sometimes fraudulent practices by certain special interest groups.

The problems associated with overweight and obesity are serious enough for adults, but thanks to an increased addiction to unhealthy sugars and fats, the use of growth hormones in dairy herds, and many other factors, we have in less than thirty years managed to increase by 200 percent the number of overweight children in this country, between the ages of six and seven. This is an unacceptable and inexcusable situation. Not only are many of these children likely to develop serious health problems (e.g., blindness, diabetes, and heart disease) later in life, but serious health problems (e.g., hardening of the arteries) are sometimes already found in children as young as five or six years of age.

Weight control problems are mostly the outcome of self-defeating, unhealthy lifestyles. Yet some people continue to muddy the waters by talking about such peripheral issues as genetics. In the meantime, there are those who make fortunes by fattening people up, and others who make fortunes by helping them lose some of this dangerous fat. Regrettably, overweight and obese individuals are going to have higher illness and mortality rates. There are however things that can and must be done to stop and reverse these trends.

Most individuals *can* attain and maintain a healthy weight if they are willing to fully embrace a healthy lifestyle. The main reasons for being overweight are fivefold: (1) *excessive caloric intake*; (2) *consuming junk food*; (3) *insufficient caloric output* (lack of exercise or mobility); (4) *self-defeating beliefs* such as "I have no willpower," "When I start eating, I cannot stop," "It's not fair to deprive myself," "I'm too overweight to exercise," and "I cannot resist certain foods"; and (5) *excessive stress* (Brandt 2007).

Most people don't need a special diet to attain or maintain a healthy weight. What they need is to *think right* so they can *live right*. Obviously, it's mainly wrong thinking that leads to wrong living. "Death and life" are indeed "in the power of the tongue." When it comes to weight control, the tongue is truly a double-edged sword.

• *Get Regular Exercise*

It may come as a surprise to some people that with regular exercise it is not only possible to prevent many illnesses but also to actually get rid of them. In addition, it doesn't have to cost any money to have a good exercise program. Although it may be helpful, most individuals don't really need any equipment to become physically fit. *Moderate* exercise should be just as normal a daily routine as brushing our teeth. *Excessive* exercise, however, is unhealthy!

It is believed that only one-third of our adult population is getting sufficient exercise. More dangerously, perhaps as high as 40 percent of our adult population does not get any exercise at all. There are several reasons why this situation continues, such as the myth that exercise is expensive and time-consuming and requires special equipment or health club memberships. Happily, none of this is true.

All the exercise the average person needs can be obtained free of charge. The very best form of exercise is a daily brisk walk of thirty minutes. Walking has been heralded in various studies as greatly beneficial for our overall health by reducing free radical damage, increasing blood circulation, lowering blood pressure, burning excess calories, staving off some cases of adult-onset diabetes, strengthening bones and muscles, improving our emotional outlook, increasing healthy (HDL) cholesterol levels, retarding the aging process, protecting against back problems, and dozens of other important health issues.

Exercise is one of the cheapest and most effective ways to live to a ripe old age. Speak to your doctor about an exercise program that is best for you. Chances are, walking will be on the top of the list. Whatever form of physical activity is selected, your physician most likely will recommend that you engage in it for at least thirty minutes every day—if necessary, in ten-minute segments (Harrar and Gordon 2008).

- *Get a Sufficient Amount of Sleep*

The reasons for sleep deprivation are too many to discuss in detail within the context of this book. It's important, however, to point out that the most common reason is found in a stressful lifestyle. One that's usually dominated by unrealistic goals, irrational beliefs, and self-defeating behaviors. All too many individuals are workaholics. Others simply have bad sleep environments or poor sleep habits. They try to sleep in rooms with lights on or that are noisy or too hot. Others are addicted to late-night TV, stay up too late or have other habits that foster insomnia, such as eating junk food before going to bed.

It is believed that about 100 million individuals in America are sleep deprived. It's a costly and dangerous health and safety problem. Most of it is the outcome of wrong thinking and wrong living, but others may have more complicated problems, like sleep disorders. The latter includes *sleep apnea*—short breathing pauses while asleep, which may involve as many as thirty or more sleep interruptions in just one hour. Those who have sleep apnea not only have numerous brief breathing interruptions, but usually also snore loudly, wake up with a headache, and feel very sleepy during the day. One kind of sleep apnea—*obstructive sleep apnea* (OSA)—results from a blockage in the back of the throat by the tongue, palate, or uvula. The other type of sleep apnea, *central sleep apnea*, results from a lack of proper signals from the brain to the muscles that ensure healthy breathing. Medical evaluation and treatment are necessary for either form of sleep apnea.

There are many other conditions that may contribute to disrupted sleep—for example, so-called *restless leg syndrome* (RLS). People with this condition experience uncomfortable aching, burning, creeping, or tingling sensations in their legs—which is perhaps due to the overproduction of dopamine—and *periodic limb movement disorder* (PLMD), where the legs will frequently twitch and jerk for a few minutes or even a few hours.

Other conditions that may lead to sleep deprivation *include* arthritis, asthma, Alzheimer's disease, back pain, caffeine abuse, fibromyalgia, headaches, high blood pressure, hypoglycemia, low cortisol levels, Parkinson's disease, and thyroid problems. In addition, we may find anger, anxiety, depression, dementia, schizophrenia, and other events that may lead to sleep deprivation. Last but not least, there are many drugs and medications that interfere with healthy sleep. Included here are alcohol, amphetamines, some antidepressants, caffeine, nicotine, and steroids.

Here are ten sound sleep reminders:

- Eliminate sleep pattern disrupters such as alcohol, caffeine, nicotine, and sleep medications altogether, as well as *refined carbohydrate* snacks before bedtime.
- Only do light exercises or light work in the evening hours.
- Take a short walk before going to bed or listen to soothing music.
- Do not go to bed hungry. Perhaps eat a small high protein and *complex carbohydrate* snack an hour or more before going to bed.
- Establish a regular bedtime routine. Stick to a wake-up and bedtime schedule. This must include at least eight hours of sleep for adults, ten hours for children, and nine hours for teenagers.
- Set a comfortable temperature for the bedroom. When the bedroom is either too hot or too cold, it may negatively affect dream patterns.
- Do not force sleep. It is better to read light literature or listen to relaxing music until you are ready to fall asleep or fall asleep again.
- Drink a cup of soothing herbal tea shortly before bedtime—for example, chamomile, passionflower, or lemon balm.
- Do not watch disturbing television programs or read upsetting materials in the evenings, if at all!

- *Stick to a Wellness Diet and Healthy Lifestyle*

As most of us know, there are conflicting opinions as to what constitutes a wellness diet. Here, I'll simply add mine to the rest of them. I believe a health-oriented diet is free of junk food and addictive substances (such as alcohol, caffeine, nicotine, and sugar) and consists of at least 65 percent raw foods—fruits, vegetables, wholegrains, nuts, seeds, healthy oils, clean water, and fresh vegetable juices. I also believe it's best to exclude meat and dairy products from our diet. However, not everyone can follow a 100 percent vegetarian diet (Brandt 2007). A healthy diet plays a major role not only in our physical but also our mental, emotional, social, and even spiritual health. Unhealthy diets and lifestyles directly damage the brain, and thus, our mind has greater difficulty making sound decisions and having emotional equilibrium!

I have explained in some detail how to have a healthy diet and lifestyle in *The Genesis Wellness Diet.* In that book, I stress that most of our mental and physical health challenges are the result of self-defeating thinking and behavior. When faulty thinking is superimposed on faulty diets, or vice versa, we, sooner or later, find various emotional, mental, and physical health challenges. And it is not only nutritional deficits but also infectious agents (encouraged by dangerously inadequate diets that nurse debilitated immune systems already weakened by other negative lifestyle factors) that increasingly warrant our undivided attention (Brandt 2007; Wenner 2008).

Remember These Points:

- It takes a great deal of focused effort to succeed in life, something that's extremely difficult to do without a healthy body and mind.
- A common source of several mental and emotional health issues is found in diet-related disturbed glucose levels.

- Most illnesses are preventable: 65 percent are believed due to diet alone and 75-85 percent to an overall unhealthy lifestyle.
- Some important aspects of a healthy lifestyle include proper weight control, regular exercise, sufficient sleep, and a wellness-oriented diet.
- A lifestyle in which faulty thinking is regularly superimposed on a faulty diet, or vice versa, makes it difficult—if not impossible—to succeed in life.
- An unhealthy diet, alone, can literally prevent someone from succeeding in life, not to mention that it is known to cause major illnesses and premature death.

26

Winners Have a Healthy Emotional Outlook

Winners know that both positive and negative emotions play a powerful role in life. They also know that most individuals, most of the time, can create their own emotional outlook. I've already talked a little about this in an earlier chapter. If we are interested in a happier, healthier, and more successful life, we need to overcome dysfunctional emotive feelings, especially dysfunctional anger, anxiety, or depression.

In this chapter, we will take a look at how we can do this. It is really not difficult to create the emotive feelings that we *want* to have. In order to do this, we must first let go of the myth that all our emotive feelings are caused by external facts or events. While it is true, of course, that negative facts or events are very often the *source* of our negative emotive feelings, they are not necessarily the *cause* of them.

In a given office, four employees are being publicly reprimanded by a rather dictatorial and ill-suited boss, who, unwarranted and inappropriately, called them lazy idiots. All four employees experienced strong emotive feelings following this event. Clearly, the behavior of the employer was the *source* of these feelings. But since the first employee felt *angry*, the second felt *anxious*, the third felt *depressed*, and the fourth—believe it or not—felt *happy*, we must conclude that external facts or events do not determine how we feel. We do this with our perceptions and thoughts. Our emotions have three parts: *perceptions, thoughts,* and *feelings*. Our emotive feelings are the outcome of *our* thinking, not someone else's thinking.

Winners Seek to Overcome Dysfunctional Anger

While it is true that our emotive feelings result from a combination of perceptions and thoughts, it is important to recognize that other variables, such as unconscious mindsets, physical problems, unhealthy relationships and/or personality disorders, greatly influence how this process evolves. I have described the physical, social, emotional and spiritual aspects of this in some detail in *The Consistent Overcomer* (Brandt 2000). You may want to check that source book for more in-depth information.

Anger is a strong reactive feeling of displeasure over real or imaginary wrongs, injustices or injuries, either to ourselves or to others. We can distinguish between righteous and nonrighteous anger. Righteous (rational) anger is assertive. It often plays an important role in the protection of vulnerable individuals and also of society—witness the righteous anger of our nation after being attacked by terrorists. If our nation had passively and placidly accepted this attack, then many more would have rapidly followed the first one. I mention this because there are those who believe that anger, in any form, is always irrational.

We can extend the above illustration also to those who are blinded by unrighteous (irrational) anger. The anger we find in those who willfully seek to destroy people is aggressive and irrational. Hateful anger has no redeeming qualities whatsoever. It seeks to blame, dissolve, harm, hurt, or terrorize men, women, and children who often have done nothing whatsoever to the perpetrators of terror. Irrational anger—aggressive, blind, and destructive—is often intertwined with cultism, emotionalism, fanaticism, and fatalism. This kind of anger with its cruelty, hatred, and hostility has nothing to do with assertive anger, which seeks to *defend* and *protect* innocent people against forces of evil.

So what about the dysfunctional and inappropriate anger that may exist in our life? Most of our inappropriate anger is the result of anger-specific self-talk. As long as we continue to demand that certain facts or events *must, should,* or *ought to* be different than they realistically are, or can be, then we will continue to make ourselves angry. To remedy this, we must carefully consider our thoughts, beliefs, and attitudes. We may find common thinking errors such as *arbitrary inferences* (wrongly assuming that others have ulterior motives), *mind reading* ("knowing" what others are thinking), or *selective abstraction* (focusing on that which supports *our* biases and prejudices).

Winners Seek to Overcome Dysfunctional Anxiety

Anxiety is a very common emotive feeling experienced by millions of normal individuals, including some who have a winning attitude and who in the pursuit of their wholesome goals, get up one more time, every time. At times, anxiety can be disabling, and this holds especially true for *anxiety disorders* such as panic disorder or posttraumatic stress disorder. In this chapter, however, we are looking at *normal anxiety*: a feeling of apprehensiveness or uneasiness about some unclear demand or possible threat to our well-being. With *anxiety*, we are not sure why we feel the way we do, whereas with *fear*, we know exactly why. The solution to anxiety is usually found in a threefold approach: developing a healthy lifestyle, mastering wholesome self-talk ("death and life are in the power of the tongue"), and *sometimes* the use of medications.

It's always important to obtain a sound medical evaluation. There are as many as fifty different medical conditions that may play a role in anxiety-related problems (Brandt 2000). But here, as in problems with dysfunctional anger, you will find that self-talk holds final sway over most of our self-induced anxiety. Often, the culprit is found in *arbitrary inferences* (drawing conclusions in the absence of sufficient evidence), *catastrophizing* (overemphasizing a worst possible outcome), and *overgeneralization* (basing conclusions on scanty data).

To overcome normal anxiety, it is important to identify *thinking errors* and to get into the habit of *self-talk verification* by frequently asking these three questions: "Is what I am saying and/or doing *realistic?*" "Is what I am saying and/or doing *rational?*" "Is what I am saying and/or doing *positive?*" Since your feelings flow from your thinking, it's important to replace self-defeating thoughts with constructive ones. Let's go back to the earlier story about the four employees who were called *lazy idiots* by their employer. Here is an example of what the anxious employee could do to quickly feel better. It simply involves making sure that her perception and self-talk are accurate and, if not, to correct this (Brandt 1988).

Unchallenged and Challenged Self-Talk of an Anxious Employee

Unchallenged Event

Perception: My boss calls me a lazy idiot.

Self-Talk: I am scared and wonder what is going to happen. I am sure he wants to get rid of me. Things can only get worse unless I start to shape up soon. I don't know how.

Emotion: I feel anxious.

Challenged Event

Perception: My boss calls everyone in the office lazy idiots.

Self-Talk: My boss calls me and my colleagues lazy idiots. He does not just pick on me. I am not afraid. There is nothing life threatening going on, and if this were so, I'd be far better off to be as calm as possible. I don't know if my boss wants to fire me. He has never said so, and my last three work performance evaluations have been "outstanding." If there is anything to "shape up," it's my perceptions and thoughts. The simple truth is that someone calling me an idiot doesn't make me into one. I also know how I can do even better work. I need to carefully check my work before I mail it out.

Emotion: I feel calm.

It has been said that one swallow doesn't make a spring. And one challenge to self-defeating thoughts and beliefs is no guarantee that an anxious employee won't be anxious again the next time she's being criticized by her boss. She can buy herself some insurance, however, by *mentally practicing* how to react more rationally at some future event. Here is the self-talk script she committed to memory:

Anxiety Antidote Self-Talk Script

I have made an error, and my boss publicly calls me a lazy idiot. As I listen to him, I reflect on how inaccurate his statement is. After all, I continue to receive outstanding work-performance ratings from him and have received several merit promotions during the last four years.

Rather than bringing my work performance to his attention, I take the initiative by accepting responsibility for the error and overlooking the senseless statement my boss has made about me. I'll look him directly in the eyes and tell him in a polite voice that I'll correct the error. I hear myself, saying, "Thank you for bringing this matter to my attention. I will correct it without delay." I feel completely calm during the entire event. As a fallible and imperfect human being, I know that it is not possible never to make any errors.

Winners Seek to Overcome Dysfunctional Depression

All healthy human beings experience both positive and negative emotions throughout their life span. Most of us know that it is quite normal to be depressed about some tragic or unhappy event in our life or someone else's life. At times, however, depression is of a dysfunctional nature. The latter is an unhappy mental/emotional state that may affect a person's entire being—mind, body, and spirit.

Dysfunctional depression is characterized by prolonged and/or repeated periods of isolation, loneliness, sadness, self-blame, self-pity, and/or withdrawal. Additionally, there are likely to be problems with appetite, sleep, and weight control. The thoughts and beliefs of individuals with dysfunctional depression are usually focused on some real or perceived significant lack or loss in their life. This is often expressed as helplessness, hopelessness, and worthlessness.

Depression is not the same as *depressive illness*. The former is primarily related to self-defeating thinking, while the latter is usually the outcome of a genetic predisposition, or a combination of a biochemical imbalance *and* self-defeating thinking. In depressive illness, we are likely to find not only feelings of helplessness and hopelessness but also morbid sadness, suicidal thoughts, impaired thinking, and major changes in appetite, sleep, and sexual desire patterns. Two common types of depressive illness are *bipolar disorder* (with depressive and manic episodes) and *unipolar disorder* (recurrent depressive episodes).

Both depression and depressive illness need to be distinguished from a *depressive personality style* or *disorder*. A depressive personality style is formed early in life as the result of multiple and prolonged negative experiences. If you have a depressive personality style, you probably don't know when this first started. It will seem as if you have always been a rather negative, pessimistic, or quickly defeated person.

Any dysfunctional emotion—whether anger, anxiety, or depression—may ultimately become a stress disorder and affects one's entire being. There are no zippers between mind, body, and spirit. In the treatment of dysfunctional emotions there has to be involvement of both mind and body. The mind must become focused on the power of constructive thinking, and the body must become saturated with healthy nutrients, protected from toxins, and revitalized with proper exercise and sleep. Ideally, all this is accomplished within the context of a meaningful and loving relationship.

In order to have a healthy emotional outlook, we must have healthy thoughts and beliefs. Self-defeating thoughts and beliefs are the major reason for most dysfunctional emotions. The way we think and speak determines how we feel. "Pleasant words," the book of Proverbs reminds us, "are like honey, sweet to the mind and health to the body." If we want to have a happy and healthy outlook on life, we need to appreciate the power of choice. There is an inordinate amount of meanness and ugliness in the world, but there is also an inordinate amount of goodness and beauty. We need to be aware of the bad, but must focus on the good; aware of our weaknesses, but focus on our strengths.

Some Helpful Steps toward a Healthy Emotional Outlook

- *Live by Realism*

If something is not true or good, don't say it, believe it, or do it. Focus on objective reality. Strive for excellence, not perfection.

- *Live by Reason*

Do your best to stay alive as long and happily as possible without making a big fuss about it. Focus on constructive solutions. Foster the art of discernment. Rationally, evaluate both sides of the same coin, but remember that only one side can come out on top.

- *Live by Optimism*

After validation and evaluation comes positive expectation. The first two steps prepare an astronaut to get ready for takeoff.

The last step makes it possible to actually do it. Focus on hopeful expectations *after* your homework is done.

- *Live by Choice*

Meaning and purpose do not grow on trees, don't fall out of the skies, and can't be bought. The only way to have a meaningful existence is to search and work for it. Focus on *what* you value and *why* you do things in life, and the beauty of life will unfold before you.

- *Live by Values*

Life is a fleeting moment and material things have no lasting value. The worth of your life is solely determined by the values you embrace. Focus on worthwhile and virtuous events and practice them!

- *Watch Your Thoughts*

You cannot be a winner in this life without the power of winning thinking. The latter, however, is not possible without your *careful* participation. "The pen," wrote Erasmus of Rotterdam, "is mightier than the sword." In reality, of course, the pen is only a tiny timid tool in the hand of its master. The pen's might comes from the hand of those who have conquered their own mind and have cleaned out the cobwebs of self-defeating thinking. Here are some thinking errors that may be found during a "cleansing" of the mind.

> *Arbitrary inferences.* Drawing conclusions or making hasty decisions although sufficient evidence is lacking.

> *Catastrophizing.* Overemphasizing a worst possible scenario without first considering more appropriate ones.

> *Dichotomous thinking.* All or nothing thinking. Also known as black or white, hot or cold thinking.

Emotional reasoning. Erroneously equating subjective feelings with objective reality, accepting subjective feelings as facts.

Magnification. Greatly overestimating the significance of a fact or event, "making a mountain out of a mole hill."

Mind reading. Elevating guessing and speculating to supernaturally knowing what someone else is thinking; claiming to know what others are thinking.

Minimization. Greatly understating the significance of a fact or event; underestimating something.

Negative memory bias. Habitually remembering negative rather than positive experiences, especially those pertaining to other individuals.

Overgeneralization. Making broad or sweeping conclusions based on scanty or questionable data.

Selective abstraction. Focusing on those things that support our personal assumptions and disregarding the rest.

- *Watch Your Beliefs*

By repeatedly pairing your perceptions with your sincere thoughts about certain facts and events, your thoughts will eventually be converted into beliefs. *Beliefs are personally meaningful, conscious mental programs that rightly or wrongly provide us with the assurances and persuasions by which we live.* Beliefs are an important part of our phenomenal world. A world that without further investigation may often seem unreasonable. It is a world often beset with faulty beliefs that may be a direct hindrance to a healthy emotional life. Here are a few examples of self-defeating beliefs (Brandt 1977):

I have no control over how I feel. At first blush, this belief makes good sense to many people. Some people still feel angry, anxious, or depressed over events that took place years and even decades ago. But as I've discussed earlier, facts and events, while a source, are not necessarily the cause of our emotive feelings. Events don't disturb us; we disturb ourselves over events.

Of course, at times, it's not only normal but also even healthy to have negative emotive feelings. But this only holds true as long as we know that we are the ones that create these feelings. Rather than saying, "This makes me depressed," you could say, "I'm making myself depressed over this." Instead of saying, "This unfairness makes me angry," you could say, "I'm making myself angry over this unfairness." No matter how hurtful, unfair, or unjust an event may be, or how we feel about it, we alone control and choose our emotive feelings.

It's easier to avoid than to face up to my difficulties. It may appear easier at first, but eventually, it only makes your life more difficult. Your avoidance is probably driven by fears of humiliation, shame, or rejection. It's erroneous to think that it is easier to avoid than face up to difficulties, but I think it likely that you may also have some additional faulty beliefs such as "I should not trust anyone" and "I must be careful or I'll get hurt."

Avoiding problems, putting off work that needs to be done, making excuses for not finishing certain tasks, and so forth, may also be symptomatic of an avoidant, compulsive, or self-defeating personality style. For a better understanding of personality styles, you may want to study *How to Get Along with Yourself and Others* (2003).

In order to feel good about myself, I must be fully qualified in everything I do. In order to succeed in life, it's important to be as competent and qualified as possible in your occupation or profession and, hopefully, in most other areas of your life as well. Striving for excellence is not only commendable but also necessary for success in life. However, insisting that you can only feel good about yourself unless you attain absolute perfection in everything you do is very self-defeating.

It is not possible for a fallible, imperfect human being to ever reach perfection here on earth. Worse, unless you accept yourself as a fallible human being and stop beating yourself over the head, you will not only make your own life miserable, but also provide an opportunity for those around you to do likewise. Certainly, it's not fun to live with someone who is holding on to impossible demands. Not to mention that you may also make impossible demands on other people and incorrectly see them as incompetent, unmotivated, or lazy.

Even if you had nine lives to live, you could not fully develop all your abilities, let alone become completely qualified in all of them. Underlying your anxious striving for control and perfection is, perhaps, the mistaken belief that only perfect individuals will be loved by others. This is often a hang-up from childhood or adolescence that needs to be discarded. It is also time to accept that the brain is an incredibly adaptable living organ that can literally change itself. There's nothing fixed or unchanging about our emotions or personality (Doidge 2007).

A Healthy Emotional Outlook Requires Healthy Self-Talk

Being mindful that death and life are in the power of the tongue, and hence under our own control, we first looked at the basic anatomy of dysfunctional anger, anxiety, and depression. Finally, we focused on what matters most for a healthy emotional outlook— living by realism, reason, optimism, choice, values, getting rid of thinking errors, and learning to watch the thoughts and beliefs by which we live.

Here are some self-talk suggestions that may help you to get along better *with yourself.*

> • I have the power of choice. • I can shape my own future.
> • I focus on solutions. • I have a sensible lifestyle. • I am
> enthusiastic. • I live by realism, reason, optimism (truth,
> reason, and faith). • I am cheerful. • I am motivated. •
> I always get up one more time. • I use only healing and
> pleasant words. • I focus on things that are life and health
> preserving, goal achieving, emotionally satisfying, and
> conflict reducing. • I am a fallible and imperfect human
> being, neither superior nor inferior. By selecting specific
> thoughts, I choose to have specific emotive feelings. • I
> confidently and optimistically look to the future.

In order to get along better *with others*, start saying and implementing the following healthy self-talk:

> • I neither criticize nor attempt to get even. • I don't
> harp on differences, but search for agreements. • I do
> good things even for those who oppose or dislike me. •
> I am an objective and patient listener. • I communicate
> on both a verbal and nonverbal level. • I use appropriate
> and timely self-disclosure. • I realize that others may

think differently than I do and don't demand that they get along with me. • I am quick to forgive. • I help others develop a sense of personal worth whenever I have an opportunity to do so.

Remember These Points:

- Emotive feelings flow from a person's perceptions and thoughts; different people may have entirely different emotional responses to an identical fact or event.
- Whenever possible, it is important to overcome dysfunctional emotions and focus on a healthy emotional outlook.
- Helpful steps toward a healthy emotional outlook include the following: living by realism, reason, optimism, choice and values, and carefully considering our evaluative thoughts and beliefs.
- Since death and life are literally in the power of the tongue, it is important to habitually embrace constructive self-talk.

27

Winners Have a Healthy Philosophy of Life

An important quality that often sets winners apart from many other individuals is found in their healthy philosophy of life. Winners habitually look above and beyond themselves and the challenges at hand by staying focused on solutions and fostering sound values that are conducive to personal as well as societal excellence.

Winners Are Solution Focused

Winners are solution-focused individuals who plan realistically, interpret rationally, and proceed positively. When confronted with challenges, they gather factual information and properly assess what is relevant. Rather than lingering on difficulties, they concentrate their energy on creating opportunities, possibilities, and solutions. Winners are far more interested in what works than what doesn't work, the present over the past, health over pathology, and so forth.

Winners pay close attention to objective reality but then move ahead and apply rational thinking principles to the issues at hand. Winners know that dwelling on problems tends to magnify them, and that excessive emotional release tends to become dysfunctional catharsis. Realistic thinking lays the solid foundation for sound decision making; rational thinking brings solutions into focus, and positive thinking provides the confidence to proceed.

We must be careful what we focus on. If we focus on bad things, we are more likely to reap bad things, but if we focus on good things, we are more likely to reap good things. When it comes to the power of the tongue, we may find that conversations we have with ourselves are often more irrational than those we have with others, by repeating the same things over and over to ourselves and speaking far more nonsense if we think that no one is listening.

To more fully appreciate the power of solution-focused thinking, we only need to look at those overcomers who, in spite of physical challenges, are able to accomplish what many people in perfectly good health seem unable to do. For example, Joni Eareckson Tada, who, although completely paralyzed, learned to paint with her mouth and became an accomplished artist. Even more startling, perhaps, is the case of Lisa Fittipaldi, who lost her eyesight to a medical condition that cut off the blood supply to her optic nerves. Although blind and lacking training and experience, she became a professional painter whose artwork is said to be found throughout the world. I know it is incredulous that so many paralyzed persons have learned to paint with their mouth, but here is a *sightless person* who makes first-class paintings. Throughout history, we find that solution-focused individuals can accomplish some of the most incredible feats.

Take motivational speaker John Foppe who, without arms or prosthesis, earns his own living and travels the country by himself. This alone is a major achievement, but he also has other accomplishments, like playing the guitar with his feet. Solution-focused thinking, with a good dose of faith, truly can move mountains. There are many others like John Foppe, who have no arms, yet play the guitar, teach school, and do just about anything that individuals with both arms and hands are doing.

More than thirty years ago, while living in England, I learned about two very remarkable young people who inspired me with their incredible courage and other winning traits. Christy Brown and Maureen Smith had successfully dealt with major physical challenges and both had written a book about their experiences. Logically speaking, no one would have ever thought it possible that they would be able to do this.

After all, Christy Brown, an Irishman from Dublin, had been disabled from birth with such serious brain damage that he was unable to talk, walk, or use his arms and hands. He only had some control over his left foot, had no formal education of any kind, lived in a wheelchair and was considered by many to be a helpless person who could only grunt. But one day, the world learned differently. I remember how surprised I was when I found an entire page in the *London Sunday Times* that had been devoted to this young man's incredible life story.

Apparently, Christy's devoted mother, who always taught her son as best she could, had one fateful day placed a manual typewriter at his left foot. It was on that typewriter that he painstakingly learned to type with his left toe. One letter at a time, he wrote a most remarkable book that revealed a fertile and intelligent mind. The book was an instant success; Christy Brown had found a way to communicate with the use of his left foot and soon found himself even happily married.

The other young person, Maureen Smith (1972), had a similarly inspiring story to tell. She was born without arms and only had the use of her right leg. Her left leg was feeble and twisted, and for all practical purposes useless. When she was about six months old, Maureen began using her right foot to grip someone's fingers and started to play with the rattle in her crib. In spite of being fitted later in life with a prosthesis and receiving various kinds of therapy, she could not learn how to walk. None of this, however, kept her from succeeding in life. What is so remarkable about Maureen Smith is that by sheer tenacity she not only became a *well-educated* but also a very *well-rounded* person with a positive attitude.

At age twenty-nine, she neatly and legibly wrote with her right foot an inspiring autobiography. Maureen Smith—without arms and spending most of her time in a wheelchair—is a great example of a true winner. As we read her autobiography, it becomes self-evident that she had the three primary traits of realism, reason, and optimism that are found in all winners. However, we can also identify such secondary traits as adaptability, altruism, assertiveness, competence, courage, discipline, enthusiasm, motivation, and tenacity.

It makes little difference if we look at those who face major physical challenges or those who face mental, emotional, or social challenges. Like the prejudice faced by Rosa Parks and Martin Luther King Jr., persecution by Dietrich Bonhoeffer, or poverty by Abraham Lincoln and Anne Sullivan. Again and again, we find that authentic winners cannot be defeated or restrained by any challenge. Real winners are solution-focused and always look for new possibilities and opportunities. And they always find them!

It is, of course, only possible to be solution-focused if we have at least some opportunity to make wise choices. Happily, in this country, most people have this. Yet only a minority of individuals avail themselves of it. Why? I think they've allowed themselves to be misled by wrong thinking—unrealistic, irrational, and negative thinking. Yet the power to choose remains available to those who decide to put the necessary effort into it. *There is no victory without focused effort.* Not every individual has, of course, the same window of opportunity. But as we look at those who—in spite of major physical and other challenges—are succeeding, we are reminded not to limit ourselves because of genetic, environmental, physical, or other challenges.

Winners Have a Values-Based Lifestyle

Let's return for a moment to some of the famous winners and overcomers that have been mentioned. Take a closer look at Joni Eareckson Tada, John Foppe, Helen Keller, Martin Luther King Jr., Lisa Fittapaldi, Albert Schweitzer, Anne Sullivan, or Mattie Stepanek, to name but a few, and we will discover that they actually have more than a winning attitude in common. They also showed an abiding faith in God and the road map He has laid out for success in life. *Virtually, all winners have either strong religious and spiritual convictions* or some other *wholesome philosophy of life.* I believe that with or without religious persuasions, true winners have a reverence for life, a social conscience, and selfless love, as well as other wholesome goals.

On reflection, it becomes clear that winning in life has a lot more to do with values and moral standards than some people may think. In my experience, real winners are truly concerned about abused, destitute, homeless, hungry, sick, or otherwise suffering individuals.

They are concerned about the freedom and well-being of all people and care deeply about issues such as equality, liberty, and justice. *Winners want to succeed in life, not just for their own sake, but to make a positive difference in the lives of others.*

Some people believe that success deals primarily with the accumulation of wealth, power, and prestige. Others think that success is doing what you want to do and forget everything else. I think Benjamin Franklin was wisely thinking of pseudosuccess, when he said that "success has ruined many a man." Real success is an ongoing, values-oriented journey of optimal living and not of optimal struggle. A journey focused on the enhancement of humanity and not its demise, the improvement of society and not its fragmentation, the protection of the earth's ecosystem and not its depletion.

True success cannot be separated from such all-important principles as morality and meaning in life, the proper use of wealth and influence, the importance of family life, social obligations, reverence for life, honesty and honor, or the sacredness of relationships.

I'm sure that if these principles were more frequently practiced in the workplace, we could finally end the anger and frustration that is now commonplace throughout the world of work. Every single day in America hundreds of workers are attacked, thousands are threatened, and tens of thousands are being harassed. Hundreds of workers have been killed by disgruntled and enraged fellow workers.

We can and we must turn things around. And not only in the workplace, but also in our homes, schools, and elsewhere, with a return to a healthy lifestyle and a values-based approach to success in life. Such an approach must go hand in hand with healthier interpersonal relationships and love literacy. In today's fragmented world, there is a growing need to work together. To accomplish that goal, we must learn to look above and beyond ourselves. Authentic winners do just that, and thus, find more meaning and purpose in life!

Remember These Points:

- Rather than lingering on difficulties, authentic winners are busy creating new opportunities, possibilities, and solutions.
- Dwelling on problems tends to magnify them and may result in dysfunctional emotional catharsis.
- Focused effort and solution-focused thinking has enabled many individuals to succeed despite major physical mental, emotional, and social challenges.
- Many, and perhaps most, authentic winners in this country have very strong religious and/or spiritual convictions. Even apart from any religious persuasion, authentic winners embrace a healthy philosophy of life that includes a social conscience, selfless love, reverence for life, and other important wholesome goals and values.

Epilogue

Winning Thinking and the Quest for Meaning in Life

In the preface, I emphasized that most people *can* be genuine winners and succeed in life. And then throughout the book, it was explained *how* we can do this. At this point, I think that it is appropriate to ask, "*Why* do we want to do all this in the first place?" Obviously, there are many different reasons why we want to succeed in life, including the need to make a decent living. But I believe that the main reason for wanting to be winners in life is driven by a need for safety, security, and significance in a dangerous, competitive, and impersonal world. Human beings hunger for a sense of personal worth that's built on some measure of achievement and autonomy, but especially authentic love.

The Path to Meaning and Purpose

I believe that embracing winning thinking is not only essential in the achievement of happiness, wellness, and success, but also a sure path to finding authentic love and, ultimately, meaning and purpose in life! It is no surprise that authentic love is the *cardinal element* underlying the makeup of every authentic winner. A multifaceted thread of love is clearly interwoven in the unique personality of authentic winners. Their portraits highlight such *benevolent traits* as adaptability, altruism, commitment, consistency, contentment, courage, enthusiasm, gratefulness, motivation, and tenacity. All these events further expand into *values-based goals*

149

such as a reverence for life, social conscience, healthy emotional outlook, and sound philosophy of life. Please take another look at this book and review these events, and you will find that authentic love eventually resolves the quest for meaning in life.

It is important to realize that authentic love is a great deal more than affection or devotion. It is *also* moral, selfless, unaffected, unchanging, unfailing, unpretentious, and wholehearted. The more closely individuals can together embrace these criteria in a love relationship, the greater the chances of experiencing authentic love. While such relationships between individuals exist, they are far from common. In fact, they are more readily found (as I will explain later) in a spiritual relationship with God.

In the meantime, there is no question that love is indispensable to a healthy physical, emotional, and spiritual life. An absence of love, or inability to experience love, or some other difficulty surrounding this issue, is often hidden beneath the specific fears that are present in virtually every challenging love style. For example, an *avoidant* person fears making demands, a *borderline* person fears abandonment, a *compulsive* person fears failure, a *dependent* person fears rejection, a *histrionic* person fears loss of attention, a *narcissistic* person fears loss of admiration, a *negativistic* person fears loss of autonomy, and a *schizoid* (loner) person fears intimacy.

The majority of the people in this country (and probably elsewhere) have one or more of these hidden fears, which, ultimately, are a reflection of their personality styles. The good news is that winning thinking—embedded in *truth, reason,* and *faith*—can play a major role in reversing all this. As mentioned earlier, authentic love is the *cardinal element* underlying the makeup of every authentic winner because it is the highest reflection of reason. Winning thinking is a sure pathway to happiness, wellness, and success in every area of life, including the quest for meaning in life. The latter, however, cannot be fully attained without safe, sane, and secure interpersonal relationships, whether on a human or spiritual level. *Ultimately, a meaningful life is all about connectedness.*

Whatever else it does, it's quite clear that authentic love is the glue that holds people together. The presence of unhealthy or outright pathological love is very stressful and may directly affect a person's mental and physical health. Excessive stress, for example, may increase adrenalin, blood pressure, cholesterol and cortisol levels contribute to pain syndromes and magnesium depletion. A shortage of magnesium *alone* can contribute to one or more of some fifty health challenges—ranging from anxiety, arrhythmia, depression, muscular problems, numbness, and panic attacks to vasospastic angina (Brandt 2007). There's no question about the essential nature of selfless love for a happy, healthy, and meaningful life. Let us see what famous British and American physicians have said about the connection between love and physical health.

The Healing Power of Love

Well-known health pioneer and publisher, J. I. Rodale, in *Happy People Rarely Get Cancer* (1970), quotes the famous British surgeon, Sir Heneage Ogilvie, MD, that "the instances where the first recognizable onset of cancer has followed almost immediately on some disaster, a bereavement, the break-up of a relationship, a financial crisis, or an accident, are so numerous that they suggest that some controlling force that has hitherto kept this outbreak of cell communism in check has been removed."

Rodale further explains that Dr. Ogilvie, in *No Miracles Among Friends* (1959), made it quite clear that he was fully persuaded that an unhappy mind is just as powerful a player in the onset of disease as poor nutrition or a lack of exercise. And in decades of professional work in mental health, I have observed this to be quite accurate. What's more, we now know that "the controlling factor," mentioned by Dr. Ogilvie is very often "the love factor." Let's take a moment and listen to what Dr. Dean Ornish has to say about the absolute role of love in health and disease.

Dr. Dean Ornish, MD, has written an outstanding book on the power of love and emotional intimacy for a healthy life. In *Love and Survival* (1998), he deals with the *healing power of love* from a strictly medical point of view. He writes, "I am not aware of any factor in medicine that has a greater impact on our survival than the healing power of love and intimacy. Not diet, not smoking, not exercise, not stress, not genetics, not drugs, not surgery." He then reveals research studies that back up his claim that unhealthy relationships are a sure ticket for illness and an early demise.

In referring to one of these studies, the *Harvard Mastery of Stress Study* (a study that took thirty-five years to complete), he reports on the finding that a loving—or not-so-loving—relationship with one's parents can seriously affect a person's susceptibility to disease. The Harvard study revealed that 91 percent of the student participants in this study who did not perceive a warm relationship with their mothers had experienced serious illnesses in midlife, while only 41 percent of those who did perceive a warm relationship with their mothers experienced serious illness in midlife.

Things were quite similar when it came to the students' perceived relationships with their fathers. Of those who did not perceive a warm and close relationship with their father, 82 percent experienced serious illness in midlife, while of those who did perceive a warm and close relationship, only 50 percent experienced serious illness in midlife. Obviously, there are other factors involved in the illnesses that were acquired by these participants. However, the researchers fully accounted for this in their study and thought that *perception of love* itself was a key positive or negative factor.

The observations by Sir Ogilvie and the findings in several research projects during the past century are reminding us of what has actually been known and written about for a very long time: *healthy love relationships are essential for human survival and a meaningful life.* Regrettably, unhealthy relationships are extremely common in our society. And this is not only found in the "hidden" fears mentioned earlier, but more "noticeably" in those love styles that are ambivalent, capricious, clinging, controlling, hesitant, impulsive, lackluster, lukewarm, manipulative, self-centered, or vacillating (Brandt 2003).

Let's face it, a healthy person wants—and needs—to *feel connected* in a sane, safe, secure, selfless relationship. There are numerous reasons for this, including that people cannot flourish emotionally, physically, socially, or spiritually in unhealthy relationships.

Individuals without healthy intimate relationships with significant others not only fail to flourish, they are also at increased risk for mental/emotional and physical health challenges. For example, they are found to have higher blood levels of C-reactive protein—a marker for *inflammation*, which is related to increased risk for Alzheimer's disease, arthritis, depression, diabetes, and other illnesses. In addition to fostering meaningful relationships, however, it is also *crucial* to embrace a healthy lifestyle that can fight inflammation (Brandt 2007). Once again, the good news is that most people do have a choice in this. As for healthy relationships, we must not overlook what I believe is the ultimate meaningful relationship: a sound relationship with God. A relationship that is not only important for our emotional and spiritual health but also our physical health. It's now well established that "people of faith" are happier, healthier and live longer!

The Ultimate Meaningful Relationship

In the last chapter of this book, I pointed out that most authentic winners seem to have an abiding faith in God—and the road map He has so clearly laid out for a successful life. However, as I write this epilogue, I am very aware that many individual readers of this book may hold widely different viewpoints on this. Viewpoints that were formed early in life—or sometimes later—as part of their own cultural and religious heritage. And the same holds true for me. My viewpoints are very much rooted in my own faith: the Christian faith. Please note that in this afterword, I am sharing some of my beliefs and thoughts without any jaundice or prejudice about different or completely opposing viewpoints!

I believe it's mainly because of my own religious roots that I am able to recognize that the traits and goals of many, if not most, authentic winners can directly be traced to the Bible. I sincerely believe God is the original, all-time proponent of winning thinking! He is truly the ultimate winner, who speaks with absolute clarity about virtuously overcoming obstacles and having victory in life!

I have found that the Christian faith challenges us to be overcomers and winners, to overcome hardships rather than be overcome by them, have dominion over ourselves and harness what's right and forgo what's wrong. We are challenged to seek spiritual control over life's negative circumstances: its aberrations, betrayals, confusion, unfairness, and other adverse events that come into our life. However, here too, we learn to have freedom from despair in the midst of perplexity, and courage, in the face of opposition. God wants us to enjoy soundness of body, mind, and spirit. Noteworthy is that none of these events can take place without the power—direction and vitality—of authentic love.

I believe the Christian faith, ultimately, is all about love. In the words of one-time anarchist and atheist, Count Leo Tolstoy said, "Where love is, God is also." The Bible makes it quite clear that God is a Spirit and that His very essence—nature and being—is Divine love. A love that does not exist apart from knowledge and wisdom. God, we are told, "hates foolishness," and warns that people, "perish for lack of knowledge." This lack of knowledge is surely reflected in the self-defeating thinking and self-destructive lifestyles that abound in our modern world. Winning thinking, on the other hand, can help overcome all that and more. Winning thinking—with its emphasis on realism, reason, and optimism—unveils that it is not only a sure path to meaningful human events but that it also opens wide the door to the ultimate source of authentic love: God Himself.

I believe that this open door to God is found directly in the Christian faith. But before we look at this, it is important to understand that throughout the ages, people have found meaning in life in a variety of ways. They have found it in relationships with their parents, children relatives, and friends. Many others have *also* found it in the arts, hobbies, sciences, sports, and many other activities, especially in working with disadvantaged and suffering individuals. Who would question that not *every one* of the more than *one hundred winners* whose names are found in this book did/do not have meaningful lives? However, I believe there's more to all this!

I am quite sure that Alexander the Great, Graham Bell, Thomas A. Edison, Henry Ford, Galileo Galilei, John Paul Jones, Helen Keller, Abraham Lincoln, Anne Sullivan Macy, Reginald Mitchell, Louis Pasteur, Albert Schweitzer, and the other winners I've mentioned found plenty of meaning in their lives. However, I am also quite sure that none of them would have found meaningful lives solely based on their achievements, however great, or their contributions to society, however important. Meaning in life is related to a sense of personal worth, but it cannot be experienced merely on the basis of achievement or autonomy.

A meaningful life depends foremost on the giving and receiving of authentic love. The latter is a gift and not an achievement; it's an interdependent, not an autonomous event. Here, I think, we find the proverbial line in the sand: a clear distinction between the natural from the supernatural. I believe we need to directly look to God, the Creator and Spirit of Love. Because authentic, selfless human relationships would be difficult—if not impossible—to come by without being intertwined with love obtained from the hand and heart of a loving God.

A spiritual love relationship with God, not unlike a sound love relationship among human beings, involves communication. To walk with God, we have to talk to God, an occasion where each party involved takes turns listening and speaking. The scriptures place great emphasis on these events where God communicates with us via scripture and the Holy Spirit. The scriptures also remind us that the earnest prayers of the righteous and all who humbly seek Him with repentant hearts will be heard. All this is of the greatest significance for those who desire what I believe is the ultimate meaningful relationship: a love relationship with God, the fountainhead of love!

Perhaps at this point it is appropriate to summarize the basic elements of the Christian faith. But we must not do this without considering the connection between reason and faith. Reason—at the heart of winning thinking—is very concerned with the validity and reliability of our thoughts, including all matters of faith. Surely, blind faith is extremely dangerous. If we were to believe everything that others tell us—or everything we tell ourselves—we would be in deep trouble. Our faith must not be contrary to reason nor must our reason be contrary to faith. In the scriptures (NIV), we read, "Faith comes from hearing the message, and the message is heard through the word of Christ."

Faith clearly is not some magic wand or self-deception, and it is not *the* road to riches and unlimited success as some would like us to believe. Oswald Chambers points out that "one of the biggest traps we fall into is the belief that if we have faith, God will surely lead us to success in the world" (Chambers 1935/1992). I'm of the same opinion as Oswald Chambers. Over the years, I have counseled a great number of Christians who had fallen victim to the many perils of *faulty* persistence, persisting by faith to keep travelling in the wrong direction, ignoring all warning signs until finally reaching the last stretch of some dead-end road.

In my own life, the Christian faith has proven to be what it purports to be—a healing, liberating, and sustaining religion of love. A love that originates entirely from God, a creative and eternal Spiritual Being with many wonderful attributes. For God is all-knowing, all-present, and all-powerful, but His very essence is Divine Love. God as a Holy Spiritual Being is believed to exist in three inseparable Persons: God the Father, Son, and Holy Spirit. The heart and soul of the Christian faith is not only in the proclamation that God is love, but also—as the Bible so vividly reminds us—"that God so loved the world that he gave his only begotten Son." Here we see directly the tremendous worth—value and significance—that God places on all human beings. And I think we do well to remember this as we reflect on the need for a sense of worth that I believe is present in all human beings.

I believe that the *love of God* expressed in the incarnation, atonement, and resurrection of Christ are the major pillars of the Christian faith. In day-to-day life, we repeatedly find that it is an all-empowering faith, one that opens wide the door to God and a meaningful life. A faith that enables us to *choose* hope over despair, freedom over bondage, kindness over cruelty, politeness over rudeness, respect over ridicule, support over persecution, courtesy over contempt, pardon over condemnation, and selfless love over anger and bitterness.

I have never found anything more helpful—whether in my personal or professional life—than the selfless and righteous love of God. It's the most mysterious but also most wonderful of all gifts. A gift that keeps on growing the more we share it with others. I don't know of a greater joy than to experience the fullness of God's love, or of a greater grace than the atonement of Jesus Christ. Nor do I know of a finer fellowship than that provided by the Holy Spirit.

However, don't think that God will simply take over our life. We remain in control of and responsible for our own life. Writing on the power of the Holy Spirit, S. D. Gordon explained that our *thought-life* determines to what extent this power will be manifest in our lives. Gordon writes, "If restrained by sin, disobedience or ignorance, or willfulness of any sort, then power *restrained,* held in check, not evident. If utterly unrestraint, given free sway and control—ah! then power manifest, limitless, wonderful, all exercised in carrying out God's will in, and with, and through me" (Gordon 1903).

It's clear that we can't have the guidance of the Holy Spirit without our willing obedience, an obedience driven by love rather than fear. Dr. Peter Reis, MD, a Dutch physician, reminds us that obedience to God's guidance, "in whatever way it comes to us," is a very important building block for a balanced Christian life. *A life of tranquility and peace that's not ruled by circumstances or the thoughts of others, but one that's tuned in to the peace of God.* Reis mentions three other important steps we can take for a balanced and peaceful life: *self-acceptance*—God loves us and forgives us and thus we can love and forgive ourselves; *self-understanding*—we can overcome hardships and challenges because we know God is with us; and the *Word of God*—which enables us to stay on a steady victorious course, as long as our mind permits our spirit to be guided by the thoughts and promises of God (Reis 1991).

God presents us with choices, options, and opportunities, but we must decide whether to take advantage of this. We all have decisions to make, including the choice of a meaningful life. However, meaning in life will remain elusive to us if we fail in love or to make it possible to be loved. God seeks us out and offers His love to us, but we must do something with it. Happily, as we mature in the love of God, we will increasingly learn to love Him and others more selflessly.

It is important to understand that although love is an emotion, it is, above all, thought and action. Love not expressed is love not experienced. God expressed His love for us and is ready for the ultimate meaningful relationship: a selfless relationship with us. And this is the standard and goal for all the world to follow. As I write these words, I am mindful of the present sorry state of the world and the great challenge and opportunity that it presents to us.

Meaning in Life versus Meaning of Life

In this epilogue, I am mainly sharing some thoughts on how winning thinking may help us more readily find meaning *in* life. A related subject pertains to finding the meaning *of* life. Most individuals, with due diligence, can find meaning in life if they look and work for it and share their life with others. However, the same cannot be said about the meaning of life. For example, many people contend that there's no such thing as the meaning *of* life. The latter simply is an evolutionary event; there is no Creator or meaningful creation.

During the increasingly dark days of the early thirties, a Dutch behavioral scientist, Dr. J. H. Van Der Hoop, wrote an interesting book, *Psychology and the Meaning of Our Life (Zielkunde en de zin van ons leven)*, in which he touched on the economic, political, and religious instability that was beginning to spread in Europe. In his book, he expressed a great interest in the work of Dr. Sigmund Freud and others in the—then burgeoning—psychoanalytical movement. Mainly, however, he held out great hope that general psychology would come to the rescue of those who seemed to have lost their faith in the meaning of life. Let me share just one short quote from his book: "Our present time is defined by a great uncertainty of spiritual values. The modern person tries in various ways to once again find faith in the meaning of life. In the time that lies behind us, advice and support was sought especially in the natural sciences, but now a modern person is with many questions turning to psychology, in the hope of finding answers for the great problems of life" (Van Der Hoop 1933).

Dr. Van Der Hoop's expectations have all come to naught because there's no science of any kind that can solve the quest for the meaning of life. While there's no mystery about meaning in life, the meaning of life remains very much a mystery—in the same way that the Creator of life remains a mystery. We can only experience these events by faith, in the same manner that we experience God and creation by faith. The apostle Paul in his letter to the church at Colosse explained that Jesus Christ is the source of creation and that everything, both visible and invisible, exists because of Him and for Him.

There is no doubt that the Christian faith teaches us that we can find meaning *in* life and the meaning *of* life in Jesus Christ, the Creator of all things, the redeemer of the world and revealer of God. It is clear that "we are not only enjoined to love God with all our heart and soul, but that we are born to that end." While the latter may settle the question on the meaning *of* life by faith, we must not overlook that unless we actively love God by loving others, a meaningful life may not be found! From a Christian perspective, only selfless love can bring perpetual meaning in life. The latter starts with a personal relationship with God, the source and fountainhead of love: the Spirit of Love.

The Greatest Challenge of the Twenty-first Century

I believe the greatest challenge of this century is for love literacy. A literacy that even under the best of circumstances will remain imperfect because all human beings are fallible and imperfect. We are slow learners and tend to forget how fallible and imperfect we *really* are. We *know* a lot about things that we actually only *believe* to know. And of course, much, if not most, of what we *know* is based on what was *known earlier* by other fallible and imperfect people. All of us are sailing on difficult waters, in fragile boats: "We know and see in part." It is wise to frequently check our bearings!

I learned a long time ago that love literacy is solidly intertwined with a *healthy personality* and that both events are the foundation of personal excellence, a subject that's often neglected in our homes, schools, and workplaces, and even in our places of worship. There is a tendency to overlook the need for continuous personal growth. We cannot possibly have a *society of excellence* unless at least the majority of people in society have *personal excellence*. An excellence that is manifested in *wholesome traits* like altruism, courage, discipline, and honesty and in *wholesome values* such as a respect and reverence for life, a social conscience, and selfless love.

All Human Beings Have an Innate Need for Significance

Human beings simply can't afford to feel insignificant. They *must* be valued by others before they are confident of their own personal worth. In daily life, this is directly seen in a strong desire to be acknowledged, appreciated, attached, encouraged and understood, or valued in so many other ways. All these events line up with the *nonnegotiable reality* that all human beings need to be selflessly loved, cared for, and cherished in a truly selfless manner, whether at home, school, or in the workplace.

Ultimately, however, authentic love is an interpersonal event—a phenomenon based not on outward presentations but inward sincerity, not on intelligence but humility, not on dazzling achievements but altruism. It will be found that selfless love flourishes only on a two-way street. Healthy love relationships focus not on singular receiving but on mutual giving. The human quest for meaning in life (and of life) is thoroughly intertwined with love literacy, and all this is fully intertwined with constructive (winning) thinking!

Individuals who grow up without selfless love or with various forms of twisted "love," and who later in life don't receive a basic education on the nature of healthy love, are among the large number of people in this country and elsewhere who are love illiterate. Many of these individuals believe that love is mostly a matter of romance, or material or physical things. Men are more apt to think in this manner than women. In over forty years of professional experience, I've never met a woman who didn't desire emotional intimacy over any other form of intimacy. And this in spite of the incessant commercial indoctrination to the contrary.

There are some who insist—at least outwardly—that love is not necessary for happiness, health, or meaning in life; but I have found no evidence for their often loud protests. Even Madalyn Murray O'Hair—one-time leader of the American Atheist Movement—apparently suffered greatly from a lack of love in her life. Reportedly, in her diaries (found after her disappearance and presumed death), it is said that she wrote, "Someone, somewhere, please love me!" This is the cry, I believe in many a human heart even if outwardly denied, repressed, suppressed, or perhaps expressed in some twisted way. Without the certainty of being selflessly loved, many persons continue to live with confusion, insecurity, and uncertainty even in seemingly good relationships. From the moment of birth, all human beings need safe, secure, and selfless relationships; a need that continues throughout the human lifespan.

Love literacy involves a basic understanding of the nature of emotional love. In a love relationship, this includes such events as affection, commitment, communication, cooperation, honesty, intimacy, openness, optimism, patience, realism, reason, respect, and selflessness. An excellent way to become more love literate is to pattern human relationships after the model provided in scripture. This would start with "loving God with all our heart, soul, and mind," and not just in thought, prayer, and worship, but especially in "loving others as ourselves." And the best way to do this is actively, ambitiously, consistently, constructively, mercifully, righteously, selflessly, steadfastly, and wholeheartedly. There are many reasons for such an approach, not the least of which is that there is no idleness, failure, inconsistency, destructiveness, hardheartedness, deceptiveness, selfishness, fickleness or half-heartedness with God!

As I am about to finish sharing some of my personal and professional experiences in this epilogue, I cannot help but reflect, once again, on the amazing power we have been given—the power to choose and thus to an enormous extent write our own personal history. The privilege to choose right thinking over wrong thinking and consequently to have a choice of life over death, success over failure, love over hate, significance over insignificance, and ultimately, the power to choose a meaningful life over a meaningless one.

It is clear that meaningful and wise choices cannot be found without the help of a healthy brain, nor can they be separated from the three main elements of winning thinking: realism, reason, and optimism. This holds especially true for the highest form of reason: authentic love. The latter is the only assured event to provide meaning and purpose in life. Along those lines, always keep in mind that in the pursuit of any goal, *you* must take the initiative. I believe this is nowhere more self-evident than in the quest for meaning. May God bless you in the pursuit of every wholesome undertaking in your life!

 A winner is a solution-focused person
with a winning attitude, who,
in the pursuit of a wholesome goal,
gets up one more time—every time.

References

Brandt, Frans M.J. (1977). *A Rational Self-Counseling Primer.* Kelsale Court, Saxmundham, Suffolk, England: Institute for Rational Therapy.

Brandt, Frans M.J. (1978). *An Inquiry Into the Effect of Rational Self-Counseling on Reducing Irrational Beliefs.* Kelsale Court, Saxmundham, Suffolk, England: Institute for Rational Therapy.

Brandt, Frans M.J. (1979). *A Guide to Rational Weight Control.* Kelsale Court, Saxmundham, Suffolk, England: Institute for Rational Therapy.

Brandt, Frans M.J. (1984). *The Way to Wholeness.* Westchester, IL: Crossway Books.

Brandt, Frans M.J. (1988). *Victory Over Depression.* Grand Rapids, MI: Baker Book House.

Brandt, Frans M.J. (1992). *The Psychology of Personal Excellence.* Paper presented at the Bilateral Conference of the American Counseling Association and the Moray House Institute of Education, Heriot-Watt University, Edinburgh, Scotland, July 1992.

Brandt, Frans M.J. (1992). *The Diagnosis and Treatment of Personality Disorders.* Paper presented to the National Council of Psychotherapists, Royal Society of Medicine, London, August, 1992.

Brandt, Frans M.J. (1999). *The Renewed Mind.* Enumclaw, WA: WinePress.

Brandt, Frans M.J. (2000). *The Consistent Overcomer.* Enumclaw, WA: WinePress.

Brandt, Frans M.J. (2002/2003). *How to Get Along With Yourself and Others.* East Tawas, MI: Brandt Human Development Consulting.

Brandt, Frans M.J. (2007). *The Genesis Wellness Diet.* East Tawas, MI: Brandt Human Development Consulting.

Chambers, Oswald. (1992). *MY UTMOST FOR HIS HIGHEST.* Grand Rapids, MI: Discovery House Publishers.

Doidge, Norman. (2007). *The Brain that Changes Itself.* New York: Viking, Penguin Group (USA) Inc.

Dweck, Carol S. (2008). "The Secret to Raising Smart Kids," *Scientific American Mind:* December 2007 / January 2008.

Eareckson, Joni (1976). *Joni.* Minneapolis: World Wide Publications.

Elliott, Michael (2008). "Tony Blair's Leap of Faith," *Time,* June 9, 2008.

Gordon, S.D. (1903). *Quiet Talks on Power.* New York: Grosset & Dunlap.

Gribbin, John. (2007). *History of Western Science.* London: The Folio Society.

Harrar, Sarí, and Debra Gordon, Eds. (2008). *Long Life Prescription.* Pleasantville, NY: Readers Digest Association, Inc.

Hurlbut, Jessie L. (1909). *Stories of Great Americans.* Chicago: Union School Furnishing Co., Publishers.

Keller, Helen. (1954). *The Story of My Life.* Garden City, NY: Double Day & Company, Inc.

Lash, Joseph P. (1980). *Helen and Teacher.* New York: Delacorte Press/Seymour Lawrence.

Liebman, Joshua Loth. (1946). *Peace of Mind.* New York: Simon & Schuster.

Marden, Orison S. (1896). *How to Succeed.* New York: The Christian Herald.

Maultsby, Maxie C. (1984). *Rational Behavior Therapy.* Englewood Cliffs, NJ: Prentice Hall, Inc.

Maxwell, John C. (2002). *Your Road Map for Success.* Nashville: Thomas Nelson Publishers.

Nicolson, Harold. (1967). *The War Years: Diaries and Letters, 1939-1945.* New York: Atheneum.

Ogilvie, Heneage. (1959). *No Miracles Among Friends.* London: Maxfield Parrish.

Pearsall, Paul. (2002). *Toxic Success*. Inner Ocean Publishing, Makawao, Maui, HI.

Reis, Peter. (1991). *Diep Water*. Den Haag, Netherlands: Sea Press.

Rodale, J.I. (1970). *Happy People Rarely Get Cancer*. Emmaus, PA: Rodale Press, Inc.

Schweitzer, Albert. (1998). *Out of My Life and Thought*. Baltimore: The Johns Hopkins Press.

Smith, Maureen. (1972). *On My Toes*. London: Frederick Muller Ltd.

Stepanek, Mattie J.T. (2001). *Journey Through Heartsongs*. New York: Hyperion.

Van Der Hoop, J.H. (1933). *ZIELKUNDE EN DE ZIN VAN ONS LEVEN*. Amsterdam, Netherlands: H.J. Paris.

Wenner, Melinda. (2008). "Infected With Insanity," *Scientific American Mind*. New York: April/May 2008.

Index (Names)

A

Alexander the Great, 64, 155
Aurelius, Marcus, 16, 109

B

Barstow, Ormond, 34
Bell, Graham, 19, 38, 106, 155
Bell, Keiara, 31-32
Blair, Robert, 66
Blair, Tony, 99, 100
Bonaparte, Napoleon, 72, 76
Bonhoeffer, Dietrich, 52-53, 145
Brown, Christy, 19, 143-44
Browning, Elizabeth Barrett, 65
Browning, Robert, 65
Burton, Robert, 80

C

Carson, Ben, 90
Chambers, Oswald, 156
Chesterton, G. K., 52, 83
Churchill, Winston, 19, 45, 63, 98-99
Cicero, 71, 73
Columbus, 106
Copernicus, Nicolaus, 23

D

Dod, Charlotte, 32
Doidge, Norman, 140
Dweck, Carol S., 70

E

Edison, Thomas A., 30, 91, 106, 155
Eisenhower, Dwight D., 72
Emerson, Ralph Waldo, 16, 71
Epictetus, 71, 83
Erasmus, 136

F

Fittapaldi, Lisa, 143, 145
Foppe, John, 90, 143, 145
Ford, Henry, 79, 155
France, Anatole, 115
Franklin, Benjamin, 19, 28, 91, 146

G

Galen, 109
Galilei, Galileo, 23, 65, 155
Gates, Bill, 79
Gestring, Marjorie, 32
Gladstone, William, 65, 99-100
Gordon, S. D., 157
Grant, Ulysses S., 72

H

Hannibal, 72
Henry, Patrick, 28-29, 91
Hippocrates, 109
Hugo, Victor Marie, 18
Humboldt, Wilhelm von, 72

J

James, William, 16
Johnson, Samuel, 63, 67
Jones, John Paul, 27-28, 91, 155

K

Keller, Helen, 14, 19, 37-38, 40, 64,
    80, 90-91, 94, 145, 155
Kennedy, John F., 91
King Jr., Martin Luther, 19, 91, 145
Kunitz, Stanley, 33

L

Lafayette, Marquis de, 64
LeDuff, Charlie, 31
Leibnitz, G. W., 76
Lewis, C. S., 63
Lincoln, Abraham, 19, 38, 40, 59, 64,
    67, 84, 91, 145, 155
Linkletter, Art, 33
Longfellow, Henry Wadsworth, 99

M

MacArthur, Douglas, 72
Macy, Anne Sullivan, 37-38, 40,
    145, 155
Mandella, Nelson, 64, 90
Marden, Orison S., 18
Maultsby, Maxie C., 15-16
Maxwell, John, 95
Michelangelo, 80
Mitchell, Reginald, 64, 69, 155
Morse, Samuel, 106
Mother Teresa, 19, 38, 40, 52-53,
    64, 90

N

Nelson, Horatio, 65
Nicolson, Harold, 98

Nightingale, Florence, 38, 40, 64
Nouwen, Henry, 65

O

O'Hair, Madalyn Murray, 161
Ogilvie, Heneage, 151
Ornish, Dean, 151

P

Parks, Rosa, 64, 91, 145
Pasteur, Louis, 64, 121, 155
Peabody, George, 19, 29-30, 38, 40,
    52-53
Pearsal, Paul, 96
Perkins, Adrian, 34
Pershing, John J., 72
Pinel, Phillippe, 19, 90

R

Raleigh, Walter, 76
Ramos, Harry, 67
Reis, Peter, 157
Riggs, Elisha, 29-30
Rockefeller, John D., 91
Rodale, J. I., 151
Ruskin, John, 83

S

Sabur, Alia, 32
Salk, Jonas E., 64
Schreiber (reverend), 35
Schweitzer, Albert, 38, 40, 52-53, 64,
    67, 90, 110-12, 145, 155
Scott, Walter, 76
Segundo, Francisco, 34
Seneca, Marcus Annaeus, 46
Shakespeare, William, 75
Siegrist, Martin, 33
Smith, Maureen, 143-44

Stepanek, Matthew, 65, 145
Sullenberger III, Chesley B., 68
Sullivan, Anne. *See* Macy, Anne
     Sullivan

T

Tada Eareckson, Joni, 19, 143, 145
Thatcher, Margaret, 99
Titian, 80
Tolstoy, Leo, 16

V

Van Der Hoop, J. H., 158

W

Walker, Norman W., 35
Washington, George, 19, 27, 64, 91
Weihenmaier, Erik, 66-67
Wilde, Oscar, 34
Wright brothers, 19, 91

Z

Zacharias, Ravvi, 52
Zuckerberg, Mark, 33

Index (Subjects)

A

abundant life, 38
achievement, sense of, 149-50
adaptability, 23-25, 144, 149
adaptable person, 24, 115-117
addictive substances, 120, 122, 127
adjustment, need for, 23-24,
adversity, overcoming, 37, 55, 79, 154
agelessness, 26-28, 64
aggressiveness, 42-43, 75
aimless activities, 75
altruism, 38-40, 54, 87, 95, 144,
    149, 160
America, greatness of, 90-91, 94
anger, 51, 57, 115-18, 126, 129-31,
    134, 140, 146, 157
  definition of, 130
  in workplace, 146
antisocial personality, 43, 113
anxiety, 51, 116, 118, 121, 126, 129,
    131, 134, 140, 151
appreciation, 83
arbitrary inferences, 131, 136
assertiveness, 31-32, 41-44, 144
attitude, 11-12, 15, 17, 19, 29-31, 34,
    36, 38, 41, 45, 48, 57, 60-61, 88,
    92-93, 144-45
  definition of, 11-12
  formation of, 12, 41
  power of, 65
  winning, 12-13, 15, 17, 19, 29-31, 36,
    38, 41, 45, 48, 54, 60-61, 65, 68,
    88, 92-93
authentic love, 149-50, 154-55,
    160, 162

authentic winners, 12-13, 29, 31-32,
    37-40, 48-50, 55, 68-69, 80-81,
    83-84, 86, 92-94, 100-101, 106-8,
    145-47, 149-50, 153
autonomous and oppositional, 114.
    See also negativistic personality
avoidant personality, 75, 113, 138, 150
awareness, field of, 100

B

Battle of Britain, 64
beliefs, 12, 14, 16, 41-42, 51, 57, 61,
    88, 92-93, 99, 117, 119, 121,
    123, 133-35, 137-41
  definition of, 137
benevolence, 38-39
biochemical imbalance, 118, 134
bipolar disorder, 134
borderline personality, 113, 150
brain chemistry, glucose and, 56, 118-
    19, 127
  happiness and, 56
  lifestyle and, 118-19

C

cancer, prevention of, 120-21, 151
caring persons, 107, 117
catastrophizing, 131, 136
cerebrovascular disease, prevention
    of, 120
CEUs (continuing education units),
    34
chemical imbalance, lifestyle and,
    118, 120
children, illness and, 123

choice, 16-18, 46, 55-56, 66, 68, 79, 81, 135, 140-41, 153, 157, 162
Christian faith, 153-56, 159
classical conditioning, 12
comfortable persons, 117
commitment, 33, 45-47, 100-101, 149, 161
common sense, 80
competence, 19
compulsive personality, 75, 113, 150
consistency, 19, 51, 149
constructive persons, 117
constructive thinking. *See* winning thinking
contentment, 34, 38, 54-56, 58, 95-96, 149
cooperation, winners and, 161
courage, 32, 37, 63-65, 67-69, 87, 91, 94, 115, 143-44, 149, 154, 160
cult leaders, 41, 43-44

D

decorum, importance of, 93
dependent personality, 42, 113, 150
depression, 51, 116, 118, 121, 126, 129, 134, 140, 151, 153
depressive illness, 134
depressive personality, 113, 134,
detached and unsociable persons. *See* schizoid personality
determination, 55, 91, 94, 96
developmental levels, winners and, 100
devoted and insecure persons. *See* dependent personality
dichotomous thinking, 136
diet and health, 118-20, 122-23, 127
"dipping-mood, dipping-sales" phenomenon, 92
discernment, 18-19, 52, 135
displacement, 85
distortion, 85
doers, winners are, 72, 74, 76, 78
domination, 43, 57
dramatic and impulsive persons. *See* histrionic personality

E

ecosystem, protection of, 146
egotism, 31, 40, 42
egotistical and exploitive persons. *See* Narcissistic personality
emotional intimacy, loss of, 96, 151, 161
emotional outlook, healthy, 124, 129, 135, 140-41, 150
emotional reasoning, 137
emotions, 16, 56-57, 60, 129, 132-35, 140-41, 158
  dysfunctional, 116, 134-35, 141
  healthy, 137
  self-defeating, 15, 17, 31, 84, 112, 114, 123, 139
emotive feelings, 55, 57, 85-86, 129-30, 138, 140-41
  creation of, 129
enthusiasm, winners and, 79-81, 87, 91-92, 96, 144, 149
ethical standards, 32, 45-46
excellence
  personal, 86
  social, 89
exercise, 120, 122-24, 128, 135, 151-52
  importance of, 124
  meaningful, 124, 126
existence, meaningful, 39, 87, 136
extrinsic values, 95

F

factual thinking. *See* realistic thinking
failure, 29, 43, 51, 71, 75, 77, 80, 90, 150, 161-62
  fear of, 75, 77
  inconsistency and, 51
faith, 17, 19-20, 55, 68, 80, 110, 121, 143, 145, 150, 153-56, 158-59
fallibility, human, 24, 43, 49, 52, 60, 62, 115, 133, 139, 159
fatalism, 107, 130
fear, 75, 77, 150
flexibility, 115

focused effort, 18, 28-29, 31, 33, 36,
46, 49-50, 70, 72-73, 78, 96,
100, 127, 145, 147
forgiveness, 57

G

genetics, 56, 100, 123, 145, 152
germ theory, 121
getting along, importance of, 59, 140
glucose, blood, 119
goal setting, 33, 71-72, 77
God, 17, 20, 39, 52, 63-64, 68, 83, 88,
110-11, 117, 121-22, 145, 150,
153-59, 161
good life, the, 88-89
gratefulness, 83, 149
gregarious and capricious. *See*
borderline personality

H

habitual predispositions. *See* attitude
happiness, 16-17, 34-35, 38, 43-44, 50,
54, 56-58, 110, 112, 117, 119,
122, 149-50, 161
adversity and, 16-17, 34-35, 38,
43-44, 50, 54, 56-58, 110, 112,
117, 119, 122, 149-50, 154, 161
attitude and, 17
definition of, 56-58
mind-set and, 57
requirements for, 43, 44
healing, 40, 115, 121-22, 140, 151-
52, 156
natural, 120
supernatural, 121
health, 15, 18, 20, 35-36, 43, 54, 60,
82, 88-89, 96-97, 118, 121-25,
127, 142-43, 151, 153
responsibility for, 15, 18, 20, 35-36,
43, 54, 60, 82, 88-89, 96-97, 118,
121-25, 127, 142-43, 151, 153
winners and, 111, 114, 116-17
healthy personality, 36, 38, 59-61,
114, 117, 160

heart disease, 120-21, 123
prevention of, 121
histrionic personality, 113, 150
honesty, 19, 42, 64, 80, 84-87, 91, 95,
146, 160-61
human fallibility, 24, 43, 49, 52, 60,
62, 115, 133, 139, 159
hypersensitive and withdrawn. *See*
avoidant personality
hypoglycemia, 126

I

idealization, 85
idleness, 76, 161
illness, 20, 51, 65, 109, 120-21, 123,
134, 152
curing of, 122-23, 125
exercise and, 124, 151
poor nutrition, 127, 151
prevention of, 119, 151
inconsistency, 51, 161
emotional problems and, 51
leadership and, 51
workplace failures and, 51
Industrial Revolution, 121
inflammation, stress and, 120, 121,
153
insight, 15, 54, 115
intimidation, 43, 57
intrinsic values, 39, 95
introjection, 85
irrational behavior, health, and, 60

J

Judeo-Christian view, 110
sacredness of life and, 110

L

laziness, 31, 76
leadership, 38, 40, 51, 53, 91-92, 94-95
life, 12-13, 15-20, 26-44, 48-50, 57-58,
64-67, 71-73, 75-80, 82-84,
87-91, 94-97, 106-19, 127-32,
134-42, 144-47, 149-62

nature of, 77
sacredness of, 110, 112-13
life expectancy, 107
lifestyle, health and, 14-15, 17, 20,
    35, 61, 90, 118-23, 125, 127-28,
    131, 140, 153
light, darkness, versus, 111-12
love, 26, 38-40, 52, 54-55, 58-60, 62,
    65, 69, 82, 93-94, 110, 145-47,
    149-52, 154-62
  healing power of, 60-61, 63, 151-54
  reason and, 30, 38, 150, 161
love literacy, need for, 38, 40, 93-94,
    146, 159-61
lung disease, 120
  prevention of, 120

M

Magnification, 137
manipulation, 43, 57
meaning in life, 146, 149-50, 154-55,
    157-61
meaning of life, 96, 158-59
medicine, 109-10, 112, 122, 152
  lifestyle and, 118, 120, 122-23, 125, 131
mental mechanisms, 85
mental programs, 137
mind reading, 131, 137
mind-set. *See* attitude
minimization, 137
modeling, 12
modest and detached. *See* schizoid
    personality
moral standards, 84, 145
motivation, 74, 78, 80-81, 87-89, 91-
    92, 115, 144, 149

N

narcissistic personality, 113, 150
need, human
  most important, 60
negative emotions, 129-134
negative memory bias, 137
negative self-talk, 18, 75, 78, 130-135

negativistic personality, 75, 114, 150
nutrition, role of, 118-128, 151

O

obesity, childhood, 120-21, 123
objective reality, 14, 19, 24, 62, 85,
    116, 135, 137, 142
oppositional and vacillating. *See*
    negativistic personality
optimism, 12, 15, 17-20, 23, 38-39, 41,
    48, 72, 135, 140-41, 144, 154,
    161-62
  faith versus, 19
other blame, 57, 83
overcomers, 13, 19, 37, 143, 145, 154
overgeneralization, 131, 137

P

panic disorder, 131
paranoid personality, 114
parental guidance, need for, 31
perceptions, 12, 14-15, 56, 61, 114,
    117, 129-30, 132-33, 137,
    141, 152
perseverance, 33, 36, 47, 71, 84, 98-99
personal growth, need for, 20, 66, 160
personality, 12-13, 26, 30, 36, 38, 42-
    44, 54-55, 59-61, 75, 88, 92-93,
    100, 113, 134, 138, 149-50
  healthy, 59-61, 87, 114-117
personal worth, sense of, 26, 94, 96,
    141, 149, 155, 160
philanthropy, 30, 91
philosophy of life, healthy, 60-61, 96,
    116-17, 142-147
polite and hypersensitive. *See* avoidant
    personality
positive thinking, 17-18, 20, 142. *See
    also* optimism
posttraumatic stress disorder, 131
prayer, 155-161
primary winning traits, 39. *See also*
    realism, reason, and optimism
procrastination, 31, 75-78

projection, 85
protective and hypersensitive. *See*
    paranoid personality
punctuality, 76
purposeful life, 35, 46, 96, 146

Q

quid pro quo, 94

R

rational. *See* reason
rationalization, 85
rational thinking, rules for, 15, 17, 20, 142
reaction-formation, 85
realism, 12, 14-15, 17, 19, 38-39, 41,
    48, 68, 72, 80, 135, 140-41, 144,
    154, 161-62
realistic thinking, 14, 19-20, 142
reason, 12, 14-15, 17-20, 23-24, 38-42, 48,
    59, 70-72, 79-80, 92, 130-31, 135,
    140-42, 149-50, 154-56, 161-62
relationships, importance of, 24-25,
    33, 42, 54, 59-61, 87-89, 92-93,
    95-96, 113-117, 130, 146, 149-
    55, 160-61
religious values, 90, 94-95, 153-162.
    See also spiritual values
repression, 86
responsibility, 20, 28, 38, 49, 56, 122, 133
retirement, early, 35
reverence for life, 58, 109-12, 117,
    145-47, 150, 160
role models, 31, 90-91, 93-94

S

schizoid personality, 114, 150
school success, 27, 29, 32, 42, 47, 53,
    63, 71, 73, 78, 93, 146, 160
secondary winning traits, 39, 41
sedentary lifestyle, dangers of, 120
selective abstraction, 131, 137
self-abasing and self-demeaning. *See*
    self-defeating personality
self-blame, 57, 83, 116, 134

self-defeating cognitions, 123, 136-139
    weight control and, 123
self-defeating lifestyles, 15
self-denial, 47, 72-73
self-discipline, 19, 45, 68, 70-73, 87.
    See also discipline
self-esteem, 75, 78. *See also* personal
    worth, sense of
selfless love (*see also* love and love
    literacy), 26, 38-40, 58, 93, 145,
    147, 151, 157, 159-60
self-pity, 57, 82-83, 116, 134
self-talk, 18, 75, 77-78, 131-33, 140-41
serious and pessimistic. *See* depressive
    personality
significance, need for, 137, 149, 155-
    56, 160
sleep, 122, 125-26, 128, 134-35
sleep disorders, 125
social conscience, winners, and, 30,
    57-58, 65, 85, 93, 105-8, 145,
    147, 150, 160
societal excellence, selfless love, and,
    17, 20, 38-39, 49, 87, 90, 96, 142
sociopathic personality. *See* antisocial
    personality
solution-focused, winners are, 12, 32,
    36, 45, 49, 117, 143, 145, 147
spiritual values, 153-161
splitting, 86
stress, 88, 96, 119, 123, 127, 131, 134,
    151-52
success, 17-19, 26-27, 29-31, 35-36,
    38-39, 41-44, 49-50, 57, 71-75,
    77-79, 88, 92, 94-96, 144-46,
    149-50, 156
    focused effort and, 16, 18, 31, 34, 37
    toxic, 96
    values-based, 146
supernatural, 121-22, 155
suppression, 86

T

teenagers
    successful, 26, 31, 126

troubled, 31
tenacity, winners and, 84, 91, 98-100,
    144, 149
Ten Commandments, 52
terrorism, futility of, 99, 107
thinking errors, 16, 131, 136, 140
time management, 71-72, 75-76
tranquility, 87, 93, 96, 157

U

unforgiveness, 57
unhealthy diets, dangers of, 118,
    127-28
unipolar disorder, 134

V

values, winners and, 23, 52, 90, 94-95,
    142, 145-46, 149, 158, 160
vegetarian diet, 127
virtue, courage, and, 63, 68
vision, lifestyle, and, 82, 91-92, 94, 120

W

weight control, importance of, 122-
    23, 128, 134
wellness diet, importance of, 15, 127
wholesome goals, 12-13, 19, 30, 36,
    45, 54, 58, 63, 87, 89, 92-93, 96,
    98, 100, 103, 109

winner, definition of, 11, 39, 63-64,
    117
winning attitude, 12-15, 17, 19, 29-31,
    36, 38, 41, 45, 48, 54, 60-61, 65,
    68, 88, 92-93, 100
winning personality,
    adaptability, and, 23-25
    agelessness of, 26-36
    altruism and, 37-40
    assertiveness and, 41-44
    commitment and, 45-47
    competence and, 48-50
    consistency and, 51-53
    contentment and, 54-58
    cooperation and, 59-62
    courage and, 63-69
    discipline and, 70-73
    doing and, 74-78
    enthusiasm and, 79-81
    gratefulness and, 82-83
    honesty and, 84-86
    motivation and, 87-89
    role models and, 90-94
    success and, 95-97
    tenacity and, 98-101
workplace, 38, 47, 51, 53, 111, 146, 160
workplace love literacy, 159-160
workplace violence, 111, 146
world, bipolar nature of the, 135, 137
world poverty, 107

Get Published, Inc!
Thorofare, NJ 08086
09November 2009
BA2009249